Developing a Successful Cheerleading Program

Pam Headridge
Nancy Garr

ISBN: 1-58518-899-9
Library of Congress Control Number: 2004106015
Cover design: Jeanne Hamilton
Book layout: Jeanne Hamilton
Front cover photo: Pam Headridge
Text photos: Pam Headridge and Nancy Garr

Coaches Choice
P.O. Box 1828
Monterey, CA 93942
www.coacheschoice.com

Dedication

To our families, for their support and encouragement to pursue our passion for coaching cheerleading.

To the exceptional cheerleaders from Oak Harbor and Ferndale High Schools. We are proud to say we coach them.

To the helpful friends from Washington State Cheerleading Coaches Association and Washington Interscholastic Activities Association.

To the best assistant coach at Oak Harbor High School, Robin Gohn. I could not have done this without you.

Thank you to the amazing people who give so much time and energy to cheerleading. Remember how much you inspire, motivate, and touch the lives of young people through your words, deeds, and dedication!

Acknowledgments

Cheerleading is teamwork at its finest. We would like to recognize and thank the leaders and mentors in this industry for their expertise, contributions, and inspiration: Bill Patterson, National Cheerleaders Association; Kevin Brubaker, Charlotte All Stars and Cheersport; Jim Lord, American Association of Cheerleading Coaches and Advisors and Universal Cheerleading Association; and, lastly, our dear friend Gwen Holtsclaw, Cheer LTD.

We would like to thank the staff of Oak Harbor and Ferndale School Districts for their assistance and support on this project:

Dr. Rick Schulte, Superintendent, Oak Harbor District

Richard Devlin, Principal, Oak Harbor High School

Jeff Stone, Athletic Director, Oak Harbor High School

Jo Anne Wichers, Oak Harbor High School Athletic Secretary

Shirley Eldred, Ferndale High School Associated Student Body Secretary

Jennifer Roddel and Peggy Lupo, Ferndale High School Cheerleading Coaches

Janine Paul, Ferndale High School Athletic Office Secretary

Vic Randall, Athletic Director, Ferndale High School

Contents

Foreword

Rarely has so much information been jam-packed into such a highly readable book. *Developing a Successful Cheerleading Program* is just the ticket for the rookie coach who is overwhelmed by the prospect of running her own team, as well as the veteran coach who needs a complete, new, and better approach to managing her squad.

Pam and Nancy place a high priority on organization and management skills and provide a no-nonsense approach to strong communication skills. One of the unique approaches of this book is the emphasis on proactive communication with both school administrators and parents.

From pre-season to off-season, Pam and Nancy give the reader a plethora of useful forms and formats to plug in to any existing program. The fourteen chapters all include sample forms for the coach to use as needed. The book's "Needs and Wants List" is the starting point of a hard-hitting approach to financial accountability for coaches.

Of special note is the clear blending of tradition and innovation Pam and Nancy advocate for every team. While noting the need for a strong work ethic and athletic performance, they also call for creative fund-raising and team-building experiences.

Developing a Successful Cheerleading Program celebrates the new age of cheerleading where "athlete" is the standard. This book is an amazing addition to the sport of cheerleading from coaches who do it best.

Gwen Holtsclaw
Owner
Cheer LTD

Preface

Coaching cheerleading is a blend of organization, communications, accountability, motivation, and fun. Each component is crucial in order to have a stellar program. Think about these activities as ingredients in a "recipe for success." You, as the coach, must mix them together to create a masterpiece that inspires pride for both the individual member and the team as a whole.

Organization is vital to your cheer program. This book is meant to be a step-by-step guide for you and your program, covering everything from a pre-season checklist to ways to motivate and teach your cheerleaders.

Communication is key in all areas: with cheerleaders, parents, coaches, custodians, bookkeepers, teachers, administrators, the school board, and the community. Communicate both face to face and in writing with all of them. Keeping in touch through verbal and written communications will greatly benefit your program. The most important lines of communication will be with your cheerleaders. Learn how to talk and work with them. What you say and how you deal with your cheerleaders impact their life-long skills and self-image. Establish your own coaching philosophy.

Communication leads to the next ingredient—accountability. You must have rules, in writing, explaining what is required for your program. Both cheerleaders and parents need to know the prerequisite and time commitment for cheerleading. Cheerleading offers many "teachable" moments. Teach the cheerleaders that they are expected to follow the rules and perform their assigned jobs. Reward good work.

Accountability leads to the next ingredient—motivation. Think about it as the "icing on the cake." To motivate, you must instill in your cheerleaders the value of what they are doing and reward them for their success. Motivate both the individuals and the team as a unit.

The final and most important ingredient is fun. Incorporate team bonding games and outside team activities into your season. We've discovered that taking time from practice to have a little fun strengthens the team and helps them concentrate more on their skills. Often, just a little break will refresh and invigorate the squad.

In the following chapters, we will break down these components in more detail to ensure that you too can develop a successful cheerleading program. This book is a compilation of 17 years of experience. It is meant to help both the brand new coach who is taking on the cheer squad because no one else had the time and the veteran coach who is looking for ways to improve her program. Use it as a reference to building your own strong, successful cheerleading team!

1

Pre-season Checklist

"Develop a love for details. They usually accompany success."

— John Wooden

Coaching involves so much more than the basic instruction of your squad. Being a coach entails responsibilities to yourself, your school, and your athletes. By being a good role model and defining the details, you will teach good work ethics. Handling a cheerleading program requires a large amount of paperwork and knowledge of policies and procedures for your school.

Your athletic director (AD) is a valuable resource and is important to the success of your cheerleading program. It is essential that you keep your AD informed about what is happening. Give the AD copies of all policies, rules, safety instructions, and correspondence. Keep lines of communication open. Your AD can give you necessary forms and help you work your way through your preseason planning. Tasks to complete before the season begins are:

- Inventory current equipment.

- Make a needs and wants list.

- Pick up needed financial forms: purchase order forms, prior approval and fundraising request forms, receipt book, revenue statement forms, daily revenue deposit summary, final reconciliation, and fine list forms.

- Secure van driving certificate.

- Request transportation.

- Fulfill coaching requirements.

- Schedule parent meetings.

- Design tryout packets.

- Make season schedule.

- Design attendance chart.

- Develop team rules.

- Develop cheer materials.

Inventory Current Equipment

You need to know what the school currently has in storage before you order items for the upcoming season. Dig through the closet and do your own inventory. Do not depend on a list that has been passed on to you from the previous coach or the athletic department (see Figure 1-1).

Whether the cheerleaders or school personnel purchase uniforms, design a form that defines your requirements. If the school purchases uniforms, create a contract for each cheerleader to sign (see Figure 1-2).

Make a Needs and Wants List

Once you know what you have, it is easier to make a list of needed items. Don't be afraid to add wanted

Cheerleading Program Inventory List

Item	Size	#	Condition	Usable	Needs Repair	Date

Figure 1-1

items to your list, too. Give this list to your athletic director in the spring for the following school year. The following items should be included on your needs list:

- Uniform—shells, skirts, sweaters, tops. Remember uniforms often take six to eight weeks to receive, so order early.

- Pompons

- Signs

- Megaphones

- Paper and paint for posters

- Mats for stunting

- CD player

Uniform Contract

- Each cheerleader will assume complete responsibility for her uniform.

- Each cheerleader is responsible for replacing the uniform, should any part of the uniform be destroyed for any reason.

- Uniforms may not be altered in any way without permission from the coaches.

- Uniforms are the property of the school and must not be loaned to anyone at any time.

- Each cheerleader will have her uniform cleaned and returned to the coaches at the end of each cheerleading season.

- Uniforms should be washed in cold water. Add some salt in the water to keep the colors bright. Uniforms must not be dry-cleaned.

I understand and will abide by these uniform rules.

Name:_____

Cheerleader's signature: _____

Parent's signature: _____

Skirt size_____   Number _____

Skirt size_____   Number _____

Shell size_____   Number _____

Shell size_____   Number _____

Poms _____   Number _____

Turtleneck size_____   Number _____

Pants_____   Number _____

Figure 1-2

- Music

- Spirit items—pennants, mini poms, mini megaphones, foam hands, and mini footballs. Cheerleaders distribute these items at games and pep assemblies to increase enthusiasm and school spirit.

- Educational videotapes and books

- Athletic supplies, including a well-stocked medical box

Financial Forms

The public school system has many rules and regulations regarding money. If you work in a public school, thoroughly learn about those guidelines that pertain to you and your cheerleaders. The school's bookkeeper or the athletic director's secretary can often guide you through the necessary paperwork.

Purchase Order

Complete a purchase order (see Figure 1-3) for everything you buy, from uniforms to fundraising items. Pick up purchase order forms from your school's bookkeeper or athletic office. Basically, a purchase order is your checkbook to your cheer account. The purchase order gives a detailed account of what you are buying, how many, and from whom. Purchase orders must have your signature, an administrator's signature, and school treasurer's signature.

Fundraiser Request

You need this form (see Figure 1-4) completed by the school administration for all fundraising activities *before* you begin planning them. This requirement insures that the community is not being approached repeatedly for money and that the fundraiser is acceptable to the school. On the form, list the item to be sold, sales price, number of items being sold, and how much you expect to make. Establish a beginning and ending date for each fundraiser.

Receipt Book

Have a receipt for all money collected. The receipt book should have three parts: one for the student,

---

PURCHASE ORDER

Nº

TO: _____   ACCOUNT:_____

ADDRESS:_____   DATE:_____

QUANTITY	DESCRIPTION	COST/ITEM	TOTAL COST

CLUB/SPORT ADVISOR   **ADMINISTRATOR**

ATHLETIC DIRECTOR   **ASB TREASURER**

Figure 1-3

Prior Approval Fundraiser Request

Name of Group: _____ Date: _____

Fundraiser Name: _____ Acct #: _____

Description of fundraising activity (List items and cost. Attach applicable p.o.'s)

Items to be Sold	Unit Sales Pricex	# of Units	=	Total Revenue
A. _____	_____	_____		_____
B. _____	_____	_____		_____

Total Projected Revenue $ _____

Describe projected use of the money: _____

_____

Beginning Date of Fundraiser: _____ Ending Date: _____

Affidavit: I understand that by signing this statement, I hereby agree to make a full accounting of all aspects concerning this fundraiser. I am also acknowledging that I am agreeing to be held personally responsible for following all the laws, policies, and procedures governing ASB fundraisers.

Coach: _____ Date: _____

Approved   YES   NO   (circle one)

Administrator: _____ Date: _____

Figure 1-4

one for the bookkeeper's office, and one for your records. When submitting money, turn in the receipt, the money, and a revenue statement to the school.

Revenue Statement

All money collected and remitted to the bookkeeper must be documented on a revenue statement (see Figure 1-5). List who the money came from, how much was received, whether it was cash or check (if check, record the check number), and the account name. Your school's bookkeeper will give you a receipt showing the money deposited to that account. Attach that copy to the revenue sheet, and save it for your records.

Daily Revenue Deposit Summary

This form (see Figure 1-6) is another way of tracking deposits from your fundraisers. The associated student body (ASB) secretary will document the receipt numbers and amounts. When your fundraiser is complete, you will have detailed records as to how much money was brought in, and on what days it was received.

Final Reconciliation Form

After you have finished your fundraiser, and all the money is turned in, you will complete this form (see Figure 1-7). It's similar to balancing your checkbook.

Revenue Statement

Name of Group: _____   Date: _____

Fundraiser: _____   Acct # _____

NO.	Name	Original Amount Owed	Amount Paid to Date	Amount Paid This Deposit	Check # / Cash
1					
2					
3					
4					
5					
6					
7					
8					
9					
10					
11					
12					
13					
14					
15					
16					
17					
18					
19					
20					
21					
22					
23					
24					
25					

Figure 1-5

Daily Revenue Deposit Summary

Name of Group:_____   Date:_____

Fundraiser Name:_____   Acct#:_____

The fundraiser was conducted from _____to _____.

Revenue per ASB Fund Transmittals:

Transmittal #   Transmittal #

(Receipts)	Amount	(Receipts)	Amount
_____	_____	_____	_____
_____	_____	_____	_____
_____	_____	_____	_____
_____	_____	_____	_____
_____	_____	_____	_____
_____	_____	_____	_____
_____	_____	_____	_____
_____	_____	_____	_____
_____	_____	_____	_____

Subtotal $ _____   Subtotal $ _____

Total Revenue from Above: $_____

_____
Signature of Club Advisor   _____ Date

_____
Signature of Administrator   _____ Date

_____
Signature of ASB Treasurer   _____ Date

Figure 1-6

You list all of your income and all of your expenses, and show any profit or loss. These forms are very helpful for the following year's fundraiser considerations.

Inventory Reconciliation

This form (see Figure 1-8) is used to track the disposition of your inventory items. It allows you to keep track of how many items were sold, how many remain, and if any are missing.

Ending Inventory Form

This form (see Figure 1-9) lists items that are left over from your fundraisers. Record the date you received the merchandise, a description of the items, the quantity and price you charged, and items not sold.

Fundraiser Checkout Form

When your cheerleaders are selling items, it can get a little crazy keeping track of who has what items, and

ASB Final Reconciliation

Name of Group: _____ Date: _____

Fundraiser Name: _____ Acct #: _____

Income   (Total from Daily Deposit Summary – attach)
             (Complete inventory section below if applicable)

Transmittal # (Receipts)	Amount	Transmittal # (Receipts)	Amount
_____	_____	_____	_____
_____	_____	_____	_____
_____	_____	_____	_____
_____	_____	_____	_____
_____	_____	_____	_____

Total Income (line 1) $ _____

Expenses (list all actual invoices/costs related to fundraiser)

P.O. #	Invoice #	P.O. #	Invoice #
_____	_____	_____	_____
_____	_____	_____	_____
_____	_____	_____	_____

Total Expenses: $_____

Net Profit/(Loss) (Income less expenses) $ _____

_____   _____
Signature of Coach   Date

_____   _____
Signature of Administrator   Date

Figure 1-7

ASB Inventory Reconciliation

Name of Group: _____   Date: _____

Fundraiser Name: _____   Acct #: _____

Total Units Received   _____(A)

Units Sold   _____

# of Units Returned   _____

Units Remaining (Attach fine list/ending inventory)

1. Fine List   _____

2. Ending Inventory   _____

Total Units Remaining   _____

(total of a+b=c) =   _____(B)

If lines A and B above are not the same, please explain the difference:

_____

_____

Units Sold   _____ x _____ = _____
                                (Sale Price)

Total Income * =   _____

*Should equal line 1 of the ASB Final Reconciliation. If not, please explain: _____

_____

_____

_____   _____
Signature of Coach   Date

_____   _____
Signature of Administrator   Date

Figure 1-8

Ending Inventory

Teacher/Coach: _____   Date:_____

Date Received	Item	Quantity	Price Charged

Figure 1-9

how many of each item are out. This form will help solve that problem (see Figure 1-10). Both the coach and cheerleader must sign it. You also track the returned money on this form. It is a great way to document what your students are selling.

Fine List

Use this form (see Figure 1-11) to keep track of monies owed to the school from your cheerleaders for either lost products or unpaid cheer uniforms. List

Fundraiser Checkout

Fundraiser: _____ Student Name:_____

Date	Student Inititals	Type of Merchandise	Quantity Checked Out	Quantity Checked In	Merchandise Balance	Money Turned In

Student Signature: _____ Total Items Sold: _____

Teacher Signature: _____ Total Money Received: $_____

Date: _____ Amount Owing: $_____

Figure 1-10

each student's name, the purpose of the fine, and the amount. Give the completed form to your bookkeeper for documentation of unpaid bills.

Secure Van Driving Certificate

In order to drive a school van, some schools require coaches to have a Type Two (or class B) license. Check with your AD and transportation department to see what is required.

Request Transportation

Check with the athletic office for sports schedules. Fill out vehicle request forms for the entire season and submit them to the proper person. All forms generally go through your athletic office. Depending on school policy, you will either drive a school van or the school will supply a bus for transportation. Also get copies of "Permission to Travel" forms and "Parent Driver Release" forms. Both are in Chapter 10.

Fulfill Coaching Requirements

Each school district has requirements for coaches. Everyone needs to have a valid CPR and first aid certificate. Usually, head coaches must be 21 years of age or older. Assistant coaches must be at least 19 years old. Both paid and volunteer coaches need to have training in their field. The state association often sets coaching standards requiring a certain number of educational hours. Consult with your AD to be sure you are in compliance with your school district requirements.

Fine List

Teacher/Coach: _____   Date: _____

Date	Last Name	First Name	Grad Year	Item	Book # Serial #	Fine Amount	Paid or Cleared

Figure 1-11

Schedule Parent Meetings

Parent meetings are a very important part of your program. Schedule a meeting prior to tryouts, and another one shortly afterward. Complete a facility request form for a classroom for your meeting location. Have a sign-in sheet and supply a written agenda. Discuss in detail the rules, expectations, and financial obligations. Distribute your tryout packet at this time.

Design Tryout Packets

Secure a facility for tryouts as soon as you set the date. Get approval from your AD. Be sure not to interfere with other sport schedules. Complete the appropriate forms. Your tryout packet should include a permission form, safety guidelines, your constitution, the school's athletic code, academic requirements, a proof of insurance form, an emergency form (see Figure 1-12), your camp schedule, and uniform needs and cost. For more details, refer to Chapter 4.

Make Season Schedule

Make monthly calendars that include games, camp, practices, special events, and competitions. Make sure that parents and cheerleaders know which events are mandatory and which are optional. Plan your summer camp as early as possible. Once you distribute the calendars to cheerleaders, try not to change them.

Design Attendance Chart

Keep an accurate attendance book. For each cheerleader, record every practice or event missed

Cheerleader Emergency Contact Information

Cheerleader's Name_____

Address_____

_____

Date of Birth_____   Age_____

Height _____   Weight_____

Mother's Name_____   Home Phone_____

Mother's Work Phone_____   Cell Phone_____

Father's Name_____   Home Phone_____

Father's Work Phone_____   Cell Phone_____

Parents' e-mail address_____

Emergency Contact (in case parent can't be reached):

Name_____

Home Phone_____ Work Phone_____

Relationship to Cheerleader_____

Please list any medical conditions, allergies, or medications this cheerleader might have.

_____

_____

Family Doctor's Name_____

Phone # _____

Insurance Company_____

Figure 1-12

and the reason why. Keep attendance in two places: in your attendance book and as notes in your daily plans. Also have the student sign your daily practice plan, which gives you another source of record keeping.

Develop Team Rules

The athletic department will probably have guidelines for the entire athletic program. You will have to adhere to those policies, but you can add specific rules for your cheerleaders. Consider your needs and what requirements must be met so your cheerleaders will fulfill their obligations.

Develop Cheer Materials

When developing your cheer materials, consider the following:

- Review the previous year's chants, and select the ones to keep. Ask your senior cheerleaders to help you with this process because they know what worked with the crowd.

- Ask for a copy of the music from the band director. The director often adds new music for the next year. Choreograph the dances. Change things around so the crowd does not get bored with the cheer material.

- Start thinking about your competition routine, and decide if you are going to choreograph the routine or hire a choreographer.

- Write out a list of pep rally ideas for next year.

- Outline Homecoming activities and make a list of needed supplies.

2

Planning the Season

"Good coaches plan. Great coaches plan every detail, based on a strong personal philosophy."

—Bruce Eamon Brown

Cheerleaders are one of the most visible groups in the school. They promote school spirit, contribute to a positive school climate, encourage sportsmanship, and support the school's athletic teams. They perform physically demanding skills that require hours of training. Many cheerleading teams also compete in local, regional, and national contests. Before you have tryouts, you, as the coach, need to define your program. During the formative teambuilding process, coaches need to make some well-informed choices about the responsibilities and duties of their team. Keep in mind past traditions, time limitations, needs assessment, and your coaching values. You must do the following:

- Establish the squad's purpose and identity.

- Determine the length of your cheer season.

- Set standards.

- Identify the skills the team needs.

- Create a list of duties for cheerleaders.

- Establish short- and long-term goals for the squad.

- Set timelines.

Once you have outlined your desires for the cheerleading team, then you and your athletes will have a better understanding of the program and can visualize the future.

Establish Squad's Purpose and Identity

This objective is the hardest part of planning when you first start coaching. Many coaches are torn between the technical and the leadership side. Take a hard look at the needs of your squad and school. Once you write down your objectives with a timeline, the tasks become easier. As you define your squad's purpose, ask yourself the following questions:

- What is the primary focus of my squad?

- What are the needs of the school?

- What are the past traditions?

- Will the cheerleaders compete?

In many areas across the country, cheerleading has been broken into two components: competitive and crowdleading, or sideline. Before you categorize your cheerleaders into one group, take into consideration the school's desires. If your team is the only cheerleading squad at your school, remember that cheerleading was developed to boost school spirit and promote sportsmanship. Do not shortchange your school and overlook these needs in order to have a competitive cheerleading team.

A combination of both is best for most teams. Competing and winning trophies does bring more respect for the cheerleading program, but cheerleading is much more than competitions. By concentrating primarily on competitions, you prevent your athletes from learning valuable lessons from the leadership side of cheer*leading*. These helpful lessons bring greater success for your team. Cheerleaders are identified as both athletes and leaders. Focusing on both competition and crowdleading requires more from the cheerleaders, but in return they develop many valuable qualities, such as responsibility, time management, leadership, self-confidence, creativity, and self-satisfaction.

Determine the Length of the Cheer Season

Every school has a different structure for cheerleading seasons. Consider the following questions:

- Will your cheer season run year-long?

or

- Do you have two seasons similar to your sports programs: a fall and a winter season?

If you have two seasons, hold separate tryouts for each season. Have tryouts in late spring for the fall cheer squad. This scheduling allows the team to go to cheerleading camp during the summer. Have a new tryout in early November for the winter cheer squad. This season is also usually the competitive season. Everyone must try out again in November. No one should be guaranteed a spot on the squad. Often, many of your fall season cheerleaders do turn out again. Having two tryouts provides the opportunity for more girls and boys to participate. Also, cheerleaders have an opportunity to participate in other sports like volleyball or basketball. Having two shorter seasons prevents some from quitting the program halfway through the school year. For the returning cheerleaders from the fall season, the November tryouts motivate them to continue to perfect their physical and leadership skills in order to make the squad again for the winter season. Lastly, if you had a problem cheerleader, having a second tryout during the year will allow you to not select her for the squad.

Set the Standards

Every program has to have structure. Cheerleaders need to know the rules and proper behavior required. Before tryouts, have a parent/cheerleader meeting. Distribute two copies of the standards and requirements. Both the prospective cheerleader and her parent sign a copy for you to keep on file, and they keep the other copy. Stick to your rules and always include the phase, "The coach has the final decision." Figure 2-1 is a sample of standards.

Many schools require cheerleading programs to also have a constitution. It must contain the following:

- Mission/vision statement
- Educational value statement
- Goals statement
- Code of ethics
- Rules and regulations
- Code of conduct
- Discipline policy—Do not use a demerit system because it puts too much emphasis on the negative. A demerit system also requires too much of the coach's time. A coach needs to emphasize the positive side in order for the cheerleaders to learn productive and valuable skills from cheerleading for their adult lives.

You also have a responsibility to develop ethical, responsible young adults. Be a role model. Create a healthy emotional environment. Respect both the letter and spirit of the rules. Teach and model respect. Appreciate the role of athletics in the life of the cheerleaders. Allow them to participate in other sports. Don't insist that they partake in cheerleading 12 months a year.

Decide Which Sports the Cheerleaders Will Support

Ask yourself the following questions:

- Do the cheerleaders cheer for all the sports programs?

STANDARDS FOR CHEERLEADERS

The cheerleaders are expected to set high standards for their school and to set a good example for their fellow students. To achieve these ends, the cheerleaders will:
- Sign and abide by the provisions of the Athletic Code.
- Maintain a passing grade in all classes.
- Attend all scheduled practices and games, unless prior permission to be absent has been granted by cheerleading coach.
- Maintain reasonable standards of appearance and conduct when engaging in activities representing the school.
- Cooperate with each other and follow the instructions of the cheerleading coach.

Any violation of these rules or conduct deemed improper and unsuitable for a cheerleader will result in one or more of the following consequences, administered at the discretion of the cheerleading coach and/or athletic director: verbal warning, parent conference, written reprimand, temporary exclusion for specific number of days, or exclusion from cheerleading squad. Coach's decision is final.

POINTS TO REMEMBER
- Be ready at all practices, wearing proper shoes and clothes for workout, and with hair tied back.
- Arrive on time.
- No gum allowed.
- Attitudes must be positive and upbeat! You must always be willing to work and cooperate at both practices and games. Do not bring your problems with you to practices and games. The key word in your position is *cheer*. Also, please do not come to practice when you are sick. You need to be willing to do what is necessary—no moaning, complaining, or whining.
- All squad members are to participate in *all* areas: making cheers and posters, creating dance routines, participating in fundraisers and pep assemblies, etc. Everyone should be given the opportunity to create. Everyone must share the workload.
- Everyone must have a solid working knowledge of all cheers, chants, and dance routines. You must pass a chant and safety test in order to cheer at games and assemblies.
- Be dedicated to the point of extra practices in areas of weakness.
- Be an active listener and accept constructive criticism.

GAME EXPECTATIONS
- Arrive 45 minutes prior to game time. You have a five-minute grace period. If you arrive after that time, you will sit out the first half beside your coach and cheer from the stands. You must stay through the entire game.
- Warm up for the first 15 minutes, review necessary material for 15 minutes, and be ready to cheer 15 minutes before the start of the game.
- Travel in school transportation when required.
- Have complete uniform, neat and clean, at all games. If you do not have the proper uniform, you will be unable to cheer. You will sit out the game beside your coach and cheer from the stands.
- Remain in cheering area during game.
- Follow game agenda.
- Execute chants and routines correctly.
- Control and lead the crowd through organized cheers and chants. Display correct and acceptable leadership skills. *Leader* is part of your role too.
- Do not socialize with players or crowd members during the game.
- Follow the captains and do not tell them what chants you do or do not want to do.
- Do not act silly. Remember that you are athletes.
- Follow coach's directive at games.
- Do not chew gum at games.
- Perform only the stunts that have been perfected. All stunts need to have the proper amount of spotters.

Cheerleader's signature: _____

Date: _____

Parent's signature: _____

Date: _____

Figure 2-1

- Do they cheer for varsity and/or junior varsity?
- Does everyone cheer at all events or is the team divided between the different sports?
- Do you have different squads for different sports?
- Do they cheer on the sidelines or in the stands?
- Do they cheer for both girls' and boys' sports?
- How large is your coaching staff?

Remember that you need to do what is best for you, your team, and your school.

Identify Technical Skills

Concentrate on all elements of cheerleading. At the beginning of your season, assess the ability of your team. Always start with the basics and progress from there. Evaluate your team on the following:

- Stunt progression (Figures 2-2a and 2-2b)
- Tumbling skills (Figure 2-3)
- Jumps (Figure 2-4)
- Motions (Figure 2-5)
- Dance

Stunt Progression

Stunts	Must complete 7 out of 10 correctly to progress to next level										Coach's Initials	Cheerleader's Initials
Step-up Drill												
Thigh Stand												
Shoulder Sit												
Walk-up Double Base Shoulder Stand												
Shoulder Stand												
Hang Drill												
Prep/Elevator/ Half												
Shoulder-Level Hitch												
Hitch Step-up to Full Extension												
Half to Full Extension												
Half-Level Liberty												
Half Twist-in Prep/Half/Elevator												
Ground-up Full Extension												
Braced Fully Extended Liberty												
Ground-up Fully Extended Liberty												
Arabesque												
Heel Stretch												
Scale												
Half Twist-in Full Extension												

Figure 2-2a

Stunt Progression

Dismounts	Must complete 7 out of 10 correctly to progress to next level									Coach's Initials	Cheerleader's Initials
Step-off Drill											
Shove Wrap/Bear Hug											
Cradle											
Floorwork Full Down Drill											
Front Spot Assisted Full Down											
Full Down											
Toe Touch Cradle											

Figure 2-2b

Tumbling Progressions

Skills	Must complete 7 out of 10 correctly to progress to next level									Coach's Initials	Cheerleader's Initials
Forward Roll											
Handstand											
Handstand Forward Roll											
Bridges											
Cartwheel											
Back Walkover											
Roundoff											
Spotted Back Handspring											
Back Handspring											
Roundoff Back Handspring											

Figure 2-3

Jump Evaluation
Rated on a scale of 1 (poor) to 5 (outstanding)

Name: _____   Date: _____

JUMPS	Approach	Form	Pointed Toes	Landing	Timing	Comments
Tuck						
Star/Spread Eagle						
Herkie						
Right Front Hurdler						
Left Front Hurdler						
Left Hurdler						
Right Hurdler						
Toe Touch						
Pike						
Double Nine						
Around the World						

Figure 2-4

Everyone would love to have a full tumbling squad with elite-level stunts and above-parallel toe touches, but if most of your squad is new to cheerleading, that expectation may be unreasonable. In your short- and long-term goals section, you and your squad need to determine the degree of difficulty you can achieve in one season and strive for that target.

Create a List of Duties for Cheerleaders

Make a yearly activity calendar. Separate events out for each month. Delegate jobs for those events to each cheerleader. Instruct the cheerleader to write an outline of the intended job with a timeline for completion. Every Monday, have a squad business meeting to review tasks for the week and month. At that time, reinforce and reward past achievements and encourage the cheerleaders' ability to continue to accomplish upcoming duties. Separate the jobs into the following categories:

- *Group Management*—Captain(s), phone tree chairman, equipment and supplies manager, uniform inventory manager, game day coordinator, team bonding planner, conditioning trainer, dance, chants and cheers choreographer(s), secretary, coordinator for end-of-the-year banquet

- *Spirit Promotion*—Pep rally coordinator, spirit sales organizer, poster makers, crowd motivation chairman, coordinator with student government and leadership class, contact person for the band and drill team

- *School and Community Service*—Organizers for Open House, Freshmen Orientation, community service projects, Homecoming, and other school projects

Motions

Rated on a scale of 1 (poor) to 5 (outstanding)

Name: _____   Date: _____

MOTION	FORM	SHARPNESS
High V		
Low V		
T		
Right L		
Left L		
Broken T		
Right Diagonal		
Left Diagonal		
Touchdown		
Low Touchdown		
Daggers		
Bow & Arrow		
Punch		
Right K		
Left K		

Figure 2-5

Establish Short- and Long-Term Goals

A team with a mission is a team that accomplishes much. At the beginning of the season, the squad needs to set goals in the following areas:

- Individual
- Team
- Spirit
- School

Once a month, re-evaluate these goals and then adapt them accordingly. When a goal has been reached, celebrate the accomplishment. Often, coaches look ahead and forget to reinforce their team's successes. What you say and do will develop self-confidence and strong values in your athletes. Reward progress, not just success. Praise often!

Set a Timeline

Timelines are necessary in cheerleading because of the numerous tasks that must be accomplished. At the beginning of the season, distribute monthly calendars with the dates and times of games, practices, and special events. Also make a visual calendar of the year's events (Figure 2-6). Post calendars on a bulletin board so the cheerleaders can plan the details of the season. Each task, goal, and skill needs to have a timeline for completion. Remember, you are teaching the cheerleaders valuable lessons in time management and responsibility.

Yearly Calendar

SEPTEMBER
- Calendar for Fall Season
- Athletic Contracts
- Poster Making
- Game Plan
- Game Schedule
- Opening Day Assembly
- Halftime Entertainment
- Crowd Involvement Ideas
- Spirit Sales
- Homecoming Plans
- Dance Fundraiser
- Coordinate with Administration and Leadership Class for Needed Assistance
- Team Bonding Ideas
- Uniform Details

OCTOBER
- Homecoming Activities
- Spirit Week
- Game Schedule
- Game Plan
- Posters
- Halftime Entertainment (Coordinate with Band and Drill Team)
- Crowd Involvement Ideas
- Spirit Sales
- Pep Assembly
- Team Bonding Ideas
- Red Ribbon Week

NOVEMBER
End-of-season activities
- Food Drive
- State Play-offs
- Pep Assembly
- End-of-Season Banquet
- Awards and Recognition
- Send Thank You Notes
- Uniform Inventory
- Summary of Accomplishments to AD

New season preparations
- Distribute Try-out Paperwork
- Calendars for Winter Season
- Competition Routine
- Athletic Contracts
- Poster Making
- Community Service Ideas

DECEMBER
- Posters
- Game Plan
- Game Schedule
- Halftime Entertainment
- Crowd Involvement Ideas
- Spirit Sales
- Team Bonding Ideas
- Competitions
- Teddy Bear Drive

JANUARY
- Posters
- Game Plan
- Game Schedule
- Halftime Entertainment
- Crowd Involvement Ideas
- Spirit Sales
- Team Bonding Ideas
- Pep Assembly
- Competitions

FEBRUARY
- Posters
- Game Plan
- Game Schedule
- Halftime Entertainment
- State Play-offs
- Pep Assembly
- Competitions

MARCH
- Competitions
- Awards and Recognition
- Send Thank You Notes
- End-of-Year Banquet
- Uniform Inventory
- Summary of Accomplishments to AD

APRIL
- Distribute Tryout Packets
- Plan Summer Camp Dates and Location
- Schedule Facility for Tryouts

MAY
- Tryouts
- Order Uniforms
- Down Payment for Camp
- Pick Up Fall Schedule from Athletic Office

Figure 2-6

Working with Parents

"My father gave me the greatest gift anyone could give another person. He believed in me."

—Jim Valvano

Parents can be your best source of help and support, or your worst enemy. You must establish a good working relationship at the first parent meeting of the year. Present a warm, caring, yet business-like, tone at this meeting. Communication is key to parents. Parents need to know the following:

- Coach's philosophy

- Expectations and responsibilities of parents

- Lines of communication

- Handling conflict

- Ways parents can help

- Information about parents booster club

Coach's Philosophy

Tell parents everything about your program, from the expectations and responsibilities of the cheerleaders to the time commitment and financial obligations. Emphasize the standard of conduct that you want from the cheerleaders. Your leadership must inspire ethical behavior and develop enthusiasm, responsibility, pride, fairness, sportsmanship, confidence, teamwork, integrity, and positive work habits in your cheerleaders. Give your background: years in coaching, education, certifications, team records, and any other information that is pertinent to your job. Explain the inherent risks of cheerleading. Describe your means of handling a concern about behaviors and situations. Discuss these details at the meeting and also put everything in writing. Give the parents copies of all this information and also have them sign a copy for your records.

Expectations of Parents

Parents need to know what you expect from them. They may not always agree or even follow your guidelines, but you still need to tell them. Your approach to informing them of these expectations needs to be positive and encouraging, not dictatorial. Give the following list of responsibilities to parents.

Responsibilities of Parents

- Support your cheerleader by helping her to get to practices and games on time.

- Teach your child how to manage her time to meet the commitments of cheerleading.

- Encourage your student to achieve academically.

- Notify the coach immediately when your child is ill. If a student does not attend school, she cannot attend practice or a game.

- Complete all paperwork and return promptly.

- Turn in all monies on time in an envelope. Write the cheerleader's name and what the money is for on the outside of the envelope.

- Attend games and competitions of your cheerleaders and help where needed.

- Set a positive example for the cheerleaders at games, competitions, and sporting events. Never disparage the other team, officials, or cheerleaders.

Lines of Communication

Keeping the lines of communication open is the best way to avoid problems. Explain to parents the best means to get in touch with you. Email is a great avenue of communication with both parents and cheerleaders. Limit the hours that parents can reach you by phone so as not to encroach upon your family life.

Parents want two primary things from a coach: to be in the informational loop and to hear good things about their children. You can do both using the following methods:

- Weekly or monthly letters. Depending on the amount of time you have, letters can be as simple as a weekly memo telling about what the cheerleaders have accomplished and what their goals are, or a more detailed newsletter with photos.

- Weekly group emails informing parents of what is happening. Always mention specific names of cheerleaders who have met a goal or accomplished a new skill.

- A team web site is a fun way to communicate with both the parents and cheerleaders. Feature photos and accomplishments of the cheerleaders on the site.

- A monthly meeting is a very personal way to reach out to your parents. If you choose this means of communication, schedule the meeting for the same day every month, for example, the first Thursday of every month.

Handling Conflicts

Even with good communication, conflicts will arise. Remember that parents look at problems concerning their children from a protective point of view. Emotions rule their judgment. When parents come to you with a problem, tell them to schedule an appointment. They often approach you when you are in the midst of practice, game, or competition. These events are not the time to discuss any problems. Often, parents are very emotional or even hostile and want to put you on the spot. Be polite, but be persistent that you will be happy to schedule an appointment with them outside of time with your cheerleaders. When the meeting occurs, do the following:

- Have another person with you. Your assistant coach or athletic director is a good choice. This person is there strictly as an observer and should neither support nor defend anything being said. Having a third person at meetings protects both the parents and you, so after the fact, no one can say things happened that did not. The third party also protects you from an emotional berating from the parents.

- Greet the parents in a friendly, professional manner.

- Listen intently to their concerns and do not interrupt. Often, they just want you to listen. Listening to their concerns, whether you agree or not, demonstrates that you care. Many times, after they finish explaining their problem, they will say they do not care if you correct or change the situation, as long as you understand their position.

- After they finish expressing their concerns, reassure them that you understand by repeating back what you heard with a statement like "I understand that you are concerned about…."

- Even if you disagree with their assessment, try to compromise in some small way to show that you want to work with them.

- If you cannot resolve the problem, tell them politely to talk to your superior (usually your athletic director). If the athletic director was the third person sitting in on the discussion, he should say that he would take everything into consideration and get back to both parties by a certain time. If the athletic director was not at the meeting, be sure to inform him about the situation and that the parents will be contacting him.

Because of the many personality types, handling parents can be very difficult. Some are aggressors, complainers, or know-it-alls. Some will try to attack you verbally in order to make you look bad to show that you—not their child—are the problem. Do not let your emotions rule your behavior. Always be courteous and professional.

Ways Parents Can Help

Get your parents involved in your program. Their support and help will benefit you, the cheerleaders, and the team. You do the coaching and delegate the following responsibilities to your parents:

* *Phone Chairman or E-communicator*—This parent makes a parent phone tree list/email list and relays news or requests help when needed.

* *Transportation Chair*—Parents are often needed to drive a group of cheerleaders to camp, games, and competitions. This person is the one who organizes all transportation needs.

* *Fundraising Chair*—Fundraisers are a huge job, but are needed to help defray the cost in cheerleading. This parent researches ideas, plans the activities, and collects the monies. She can organize the other parents to help with the fundraisers.

* *Party Chair*—She coordinates squad-bonding activities throughout the year. Ideas are slumber parties, holiday parties, meals before the games, tailgate parties, and end-of-the-year party.

* *Snack Parent*—Provides nutritional snacks at games and competitions.

* *Publicity Chair*—Writes and distributes press releases about the squad to the local media. She

calls upon the local media to do stories about the cheerleaders. She also finds places for the squad to perform or volunteer in the community.

* *Competition Parent*—This person gets information about all the competitions, completes the needed paperwork, and keeps a copy of the music needed for each routine. She also sends information to parents about the competitions, entry fees, and spectator fees. She makes and distributes a list of the items the cheerleaders need to bring to all competitions.

* *Scrapbook Chair*—She collects photos from the cheerleaders during the year, memorabilia from each event, and makes a scrapbook for the end-of-the-year party. She can make color copies for the cheerleaders if the parents wish to pay for the cost.

* *Videographer*—This parent tapes all events and makes a video for the last party of the year.

* *Photographer*—She takes photos throughout the year. She coordinates with the scrapbook chair.

Parents Booster Club

A valuable addition to your program is a parents booster club. Forming this club will help to defray cheerleading expenses, build support for your cheer program, and encourage interaction with parents and cheerleaders. The first step on your agenda is to get approval for the formation of this organization through your school district. The school will often have guidelines and requirements for a booster club (see Figure 3-1). Setting up the club will involve the following:

* Writing a statement of purpose

* Establishing club bylaws

* Assigning responsibilities

* Electing officers

* Opening a bank account

Booster Club Requirements

Incorporated booster clubs shall be separate and distinct entities for both state sales tax purposes and federal income tax purposes. The booster clubs shall be responsible for filing all tax returns with respect to money generated and spent by the booster clubs. Accounts controlled by booster clubs, PTAs, or other outside organizations shall normally be handled through separate bank accounts under the name, tax identification number, and complete control of the organization. These accounts and their records normally shall not be maintained by school personnel, or on District property.

After filing the appropriate forms with the Secretary of State and the Internal Revenue Service, the booster clubs shall maintain their tax-exempt status, and the contributions to the booster clubs shall continue to be deductible by the donors. Each booster club shall have Articles of Incorporation, Bylaws, directors, officers, minutes book, and accounting records.

Funds collected from non-student activities may be deposited in a separate account only by organizations with tax exempt or 501(c)(3) status or organizations with a tax ID number and bylaws and financial controls approved by the principal or designee.

All fundraising activities by any organization that utilizes students directly in the solicitation of funds or utilizes the school name or school community in the promotion of the activity shall receive prior approval of the principal. A prior written agreement shall evidence the proposed purpose of the allocation of expected gross profits minus expenses.

All funds collected through school-sponsored activities shall be expended for the purposes in the approved prior agreement or for other student or school benefits mutually agreed upon by the sponsor and the principal reflected in the minutes of the organization on file with the deposit.

Booster and other non-tax exempt of 501(c)(3) organizations shall provide a complete annual financial report following the close of the fiscal year to the principal. Tax exempt and 501(c)(3) organizations that raise more than $5,000 in a year shall provide the principal with a copy of their required annual financial audit, financial report, or tax return.

Figure 3-1

Meetings should be kept to a minimum and should always have a written agenda. These meetings are business, not social gatherings. Keep them brief: cover the business and send the parents home. Parents are volunteering their time and most of the work can be done independent of the business meeting.

Projects that a booster club can cover include the following:

- Committees for fundraising projects

- Helping with transportation

- Helping with Homecoming activities

- Running competitions

- Parent support group at games

- Any of the ideas previously listed under "Ways Parents Can Help"

Remember: a well-organized, effective booster club can improve your program and give you more time to do what you do best—coach.

4

Tryouts

"You must learn how to hold a team together. You must lift some up, calm others down, until finally they've got one heartbeat. Then you've got yourself a team."

—Bear Bryant

Tryouts are an exciting, yet stressful, time, with so much to do and plan. This chapter will cover your options. Be sure that your tryout procedures and scoring reflect the needs of the entire program. From start to finish, planning takes one to two months. Considerations are the following:

- Timeframe for tryouts

- Number of days for tryouts

- Qualifications to make the cheerleading squad

- Publicizing tryouts

- Pre-tryout meeting

- Method of selection

- Tryout material

- Outline for tryouts

- Scoring and evaluations

- Means of notification

Timeframe for Tryouts

Deciding when to hold your tryouts is the first thing on the agenda. Check with your school to see if a timeframe has already been set for cheerleading tryouts. Often, you have some leeway to determine the week and date. Most tryouts are held in the springtime between March and the end of the school year. An important factor to consider when selecting a date and time is to not interfere with current sports. You need to maintain good relations with other coaches, so do not schedule your tryouts during their practice or game times. Advise administrators and coaches of your plans. The added bonus of having your tryouts in the spring is that most of the sports for spring are outside. The only thing that might hamper your use of the gym is rained-out practices when spring sport teams might move into the gym. Consider having your tryouts in the evening, so students who do spring sports can still participate.

One of the most practical times to hold tryouts is before your school's spring break. The candidates put so much energy and emotion into the tryout process, but unfortunately not all of them will make the squad. Having tryouts before the break allows the candidates to recover from their disappointment during the time off, before they have to face the student body. Another reason for having an early spring tryout is that you can order your uniforms and receive them in time for summer camp.

Reserve your gym space as soon as you know the dates of your tryouts. If you have trouble getting your high school gym, check into your elementary or middle school gyms, which are often easier to reserve. Once you decide when to have your tryouts, display posters around school to inform the students. Also announce dates and times on the PA system.

Number of Days for Tryouts

A lot of coaches differ on this topic. You need to explore different sources and find what works best for you, your program, and the students. Tryouts usually last from three to five days, for two to three hours a day. First, decide on the qualifications and the material the candidates will need to learn; then you will have a better feel for the number of needed days for your tryouts.

Qualifications to Make the Cheerleading Squad

The following factors are needed to form a cohesive, well-skilled, team-oriented cheer squad:

• *Coachability*—Is the student open to instruction? Is she capable of growing and trying to achieve more as a cheerleader?

• *Character*—Is she the type of person you want to represent your school?

• *Academics*—Is this student as committed to the classroom as she is to cheerleading? Does she know how to manage her time between the commitments of cheerleading and schoolwork?

• *Growth Potential*—Is the student willing to try new things? Does she believe she can do it? Is she willing to try?

• *Talent*—Does the student possess the ability and athleticism needed for cheerleading?

• *Age*—What grades will you allow to try out for varsity and junior varsity?

Publicizing Your Tryouts

It is essential that you get the word out to all potential candidates. You need to sell your program in order to have a quality squad. Some ways to recruit include the following:

• Place posters in the hallways of both the high school and feeder junior high/middle schools.

• Have announcements made on the PA system of both the high school and feeder junior high/middle schools.

• Advertise in the sport section of your local newspaper.

• Write an article for the school newspaper.

• List the tryouts in the daily school bulletin.

• Hold a cheerleading clinic before tryouts.

• Take a group of past cheerleaders to junior high and middle schools for a demonstration and to answer questions.

• Hand out flyers.

• Place flyers and posters in the community.

• Have veteran cheerleaders spread the word. Word of mouth can be your best recruitment tool.

• Talk to students who you think would make good cheerleaders. Often a little encouragement is all it takes to convince someone to try out.

• Hold a pre-tryout meeting.

Pre-Tryout Meeting

Schedule a pre-tryout meeting two to three weeks prior to tryouts for both prospective cheerleaders and parents (see Figure 4-1.) Distribute the following material at the meeting:

• Cover letter explaining tryouts (Figure 4-2)

• Letter to parents explaining time and financial obligations (Figure 4-3)

• Cheerleader's rules (Figure 4-4)

• Parent permission slip (Figure 4-5)

• Parent release form (Figure 4-6)

• Tryout application (Figure 4-7)

Pre-Tryout Meeting	**Cover Letter**
• State objectives of the program. Outline how you plan to accomplish your objectives. Discuss what type of program you will have: co-ed/all-girl and size of squad. • Discuss your coaching philosophy. • Introduce your staff. • Have parents introduce themselves. • Outline team rules, procedures, athletic code, required paperwork, and requirements of cheerleaders. • Outline financial obligations. • Distribute monthly calendars that include practice schedule, games, and special events. • Outline where parents can help and support. • Discuss sportsmanship for both cheerleaders and parents. • Discuss tryout clothing/appearance rules: appropriate attire, hair pulled back, and no jewelry. • Establish a clear line of communication between parents and coach. • Include a question-and-answer period.	Dear Potential Cheerleader, We would like to welcome you to the _____ Cheer Tryouts. Tryouts can be a fun, but exhausting, time. All the information in this packet must be completed and returned to the coach's mailbox in the workroom by _____. *Qualifications* • Coachability: Are you open to instruction? Are you capable of growing and trying to achieve more as a cheerleader? • Character: Are you the type of person we would be proud to have represent our school? • Academics: Are you as committed to the classroom as you are to being a member of the cheer squad? Are you struggling with grades now? How is your attendance and attitude in class? • Growth Potential: Are you willing to try new things? Do you believe you can do it? • Talent: Do you possess a special ability and athleticism? Are you in good physical condition? Tryout Dates: Time: Location:

Figure 4-1

Figure 4-2

• Tryout questions (Figure 4-8). A coach can learn much about a person's personality through the use of this questionnaire.

• Season requirements (Figure 4-9). This paper includes a brief outline of what is required for your tryouts, plus the obligations of the season.

• Physical form. This form must be completed by a doctor. Every year, an athlete must have a general physical to participate in any sport, including cheerleading.

• School's athletic contract. Each school has rules that prohibit athletes from using alcohol and drugs. Included in the contract is a code of conduct. Explain this contract and have your cheerleaders sign it.

• Staff evaluation form (Figure 4-10). Some schools use this form and others do not. It helps to have an assessment of leadership. You should decide if you think this form is necessary based on your program.

• Coach's evaluation (Figure 4-11). This form is needed if the coach decides to use the combination selection method for tryouts (see following section).

• Judging form

• Poster paper to make a spirit sign. Having each candidate make a sign is an easy way to have all your spirit posters done before the season begins.

Dear Parents,
Please read the information below in order to understand the time required and the financial commitment of your child if she makes the cheer squad.

Uniform cost (approximate): $375.00
Camp (fundraised): $200.00
$575.00

Deposit of $50.00 is due by_____ (the date we order the new uniforms). Payments of $50.00 per month are due from April to August. The balance of the uniform cost is due for football cheer by September 15. Wrestling and basketball cheer have until November 30 to pay their balance.

Hours involved:
Wrestling Cheer

Practice times:	135 hours
Cheer camp:	50 hours
Cheer and travel times:	193 hours
Fundraising:	37 hours
Time together:	415 hours

Football Cheer

Practice times:	165 hours
Cheer camp:	50 hours
Cheer and travel times:	65 hours
Fundraising:	32 hours
Time together:	312 hours

Basketball Cheer

Practice time:	135 hours
Cheer camp:	50 hours
Cheer and travel time:	120 hours
Fundraising:	32 hours
Time together:	337 hours

As you can see, cheer takes a lot of time. During this period, your student still needs to maintain her academics.

Figure 4-3

Cheerleader's Rules

Follow the athletic code and school rules.

Participate in all mandatory fundraisers.

Attend summer camp.

Treat others with respect at all times.

Always show good sportsmanship.

Maintain passing grades in all your classes. If you are failing a class, you must attend the required amount of study tables per week until you are passing. You cannot cheer if you do not.

Be on time and ready—for school, for class, for practice, and for all events you are required to attend. Leave any bad attitudes at the door.

Figure 4-4

Explain each form and the timeline for returning paperwork to the coach. Most schools require that all forms are completed and returned by the first day of tryouts. Remember that this meeting is the time to sell your program. Explain your goals and commitment to cheerleading.

Method of Selection

Coach's Pick

You choose your team yourself with no outside help. Selecting your own squad has many benefits. You set the guidelines. Because you watch them all week during practices, you can see how well they work together. A disadvantage of this method is some parents believe a coach does not have the ability to choose a squad based on skill and merit and she will only pick her favorites. Often, parents will go "above your head" to your athletic director if their daughter does not make the squad. Confirm with your school administrator that you can pick your own squad before you decide to do it. Inform both the

---

Parent Permission for Cheerleader Tryouts

Football Cheer
Wrestling Cheer
Basketball Cheer
Competition Cheer

Dear Parents,
Your child is interested in becoming a member of the _____High Cheer Squad. If she makes the squad, your child must assume specific responsibilities and obligations in order to qualify for and remain part of the squad.

After reading the attached information and fully understanding the rules and regulations which govern this program, and after your child has complete understanding of her responsibilities, please sign and have your child sign and return this form to the cheer coaches on the first day of practice.

The approximate cost of the uniform is $350.00 to $450.00. The cheerleaders will be given a chance to fundraise money for this at summer car washes and by getting sponsors for the football poster. These fundraisers are optional. If, for some reason, your child is not able to cheer after making the squad and ordering the uniform, you are still responsible for paying the full cost. Mandatory fundraisers for all cheerleaders are: Mini Cheer Camp (during football season), Tolo, and Grub Tolo. All cheerleaders must help. These fundraisers bring in the money we use for summer camp and operating costs throughout the year. Summer camp attendance is mandatory. It is one of the most important weeks for the cheerleaders, as we build on what they learn here throughout the year.

Being a member of the _____ High Cheer Squad has many rewards and is a valuable experience. It also means a lot of hard work and long hours. If a student is already struggling with grades, please think hard about this decision. Because of the time involved, cheerleading puts an extra burden on students to keep their grades up. If they are failing a class, they cannot cheer unless they are attending the required amount of study tables per week.

Parent signature:_____
Date: _____
Cheer candidate signature:_____
Date: _____

Figure 4-5

cheerleaders and parents that you will be choosing the squad. Have them sign a written statement that they understand this policy and will abide by the decision.

Panel of Judges

Hire outside coaches and teachers to judge. Be sure to complete the necessary request form for payment of your judges from the cheerleaders' school account. The obvious advantage is the panel is unbiased and judge solely on what they see at tryouts. Disadvantage is the selection is based on a one-time viewing and judges may not know the coachability and teamwork potential of a candidate.

Combination Method

Coach scores the students during the practice process, and then the panel judges on tryout day. Combine the two sets of scores to select your team.

Each of the different styles of judging has pros and cons. It will depend on your personality and coaching style as to which one you should choose. If you are an experienced coach and know exactly what you want, then the coach's pick will work nicely for you. If you are a new coach or if you have a son or daughter trying out for your squad, it would probably be best to leave it up to qualified judges. You can ask other coaches in your league to judge. If you have a

Parent Release Form

Name: _____ Date: _____

School: _____

Grade (this year): _____

I, the undersigned, have read and fully understand the rules and regulations which will govern my son/daughter if he/she is chosen to represent _____ as a cheerleader/mascot. I understand the dangers involved due to the nature of the sport. I further understand that this is an extracurricular activity and that attendance at all practices, games, special functions, fundraisers, and summer camp is a requirement of the selected cheerleader/mascot.

I hereby give my consent to my son/daughter, _____

_____ to try out for cheerleader at _____ and recognize his/her responsibilities and requirements as a leader of his/her school. I understand that, if chosen, my son/daughter will be required to pay for cheer camp and a uniform.

Parent signature: _____

Address: _____

Home phone: _____

Work phone: _____

If I am selected as a cheerleader/mascot at _____, I shall fulfill the requirements to the best of my ability as set forth in the Cheerleader/Mascot Policies and the Co-Curricular Athletic Code. I have read these policies and understand that if I fail to maintain these rules, I will be removed from my position.

Candidate's signature: _____

Address: _____

Student's phone: _____

Figure 4-6

college in your area, try asking some of their cheerleaders to judge. The most popular way to judge tryouts is the combination coach/panel process. If you choose this method and want a major say in who makes your squad, set up a point system to weigh heavily on your scores. Remember that you are the coach and the one who will work with them all year.

Selecting Tryout Material

Keep it simple! Do not make your tryouts a long, drawn-out process. Have senior cheerleaders choreograph and teach the material. Tryouts usually include a dance, a cheer, an interview, and demonstration of jumps, basic stunting, and tumbling.

Cheer Tryout Application

Name: _____ Phone: _____

Address: _____

Father: _____ Mother: _____

Employer: _____ Employer: _____

Business Phone: _____ Business Phone: _____

Doctor: _____ Dr. Phone: _____

Insurance Co. _____ Policy #: _____

Overall GPA: _____Birthday: _____ Shoe size: _____

I, _____, have read all the rules and regulations which govern the _____ High School Cheerleaders. As a representative of my school, I understand these rules and I agree to abide by them if selected as a cheerleader for the _____ school year.

Signature: _____

Personal Information:

Are you currently taking any medications? If so, please list.

Are you currently allergic to anything (medication, foods, etc.)? If so, please list.

Are you currently a member of any club, organization, or team that would require practice time? If yes, please explain.

List any honors you have received while in school.

We understand that personal insurance must cover our son/daughter. We give permission for our child to receive medical attention in the event that we cannot be present or reached for any reason.

Parent signature: _____ Date: _____

Figure 4-7

Don't have the candidates make up their own cheer and dance. Teach everyone the same thing. You will be able to tell if they have potential by the second eight-count of a dance. Some will shine right from the start and others will need to work a little harder. They might not be perfect, but you want to see that sparkle and excitement.

Outline for Tryouts

- Gather all paperwork at the beginning.

- Take roll. Have a sign-in sheet each day for documentation.

Cheerleader Tryout Questions

Why is cheerleading important to your school?

What is the most important value that a cheerleader should have?

Why are you trying out for cheer?

What will you contribute to the cheerleading squad?

What is a new tradition the cheerleaders should create?

What do you say if someone tells you that cheerleading is not a sport?

How do you calm a rowdy crowd?

How would you handle a fellow cheerleader who spreads bad rumors about you?

What goals would you have for the squad?

Do you have any other comments regarding becoming a cheerleader?

Figure 4-8

Season Requirements

Tryouts for the _____ Cheerleading Squad for the fall season will be held _____. Girls and boys in grades 8 through 11 are eligible. Tryouts will take place in the _____ gym each day from 3 to 5:30 p.m.

All girls trying out are required to learn the following:
- Cheers/Chants
- Dances
- Stunting
- Jumps

All boys trying out are required to learn the following:
- Stunting
- Jumps
- Cheers/Chants
- Tumbling

The coaches make selections. A list will be posted on the final day of tryouts. Eighth graders through juniors are eligible for varsity; eighth graders through sophomores are eligible for JV.

SEASON REQUIREMENTS
- All cheerleaders have to abide by the athletic code. This is a 12-month policy.
- Cheerleaders need to maintain passing grades in all classes at all times.
- Attendance at all practices is required.
- Cheerleaders cheer at football, soccer, and volleyball games for the fall season.
- All cheerleaders are required to participate in fundraisers, assemblies, and community events deemed required by the coach.
- Competition participation is required.
- All cheerleaders are required to have a current physical (within the past year) and a signed emergency medical form.
- Cheerleaders must pass safety and chant tests.
- Cheerleading is a sport, therefore cheerleaders cannot participate in other sports during the season (volleyball, soccer, football, swimming, cross-country).

Figure 4-9

| **Staff Evaluation** | | | | | | | |
| Rated on a scale of 1 to 5: 1 = very poor; 2 = poor; 3 = average; 4 = good; 5 = excellent | | | | | | | |
Name	Dependability	Leadership	Attitude	Cooperation	Courtesy	Grades	Comments

Dear Staff,
The students listed above have applied for a position on the cheerleading squad. This activity/sport requires dependability, teamwork, leadership, a positive attitude, cooperation, and courtesy. Please rate each student on a scale of 1 to 5 (1 being the lowest, someone you do not think would be a good cheer candidate, and 5 being someone you think would be a good role model and cheerleader). If you give someone a rating of 1, please give a brief explanation why. Thank you so much for your input. It will help us out immensely.

Figure 4-10

- Preview all tryout material (cheer/chant, list of interview questions, tumbling requirements, dance, jumps, stunt requirements).

- Review score sheets.

- Warm up all participants.

- Have extra copies of the music for cheerleaders to buy.

- Teach material step by step, breaking it into sections.

- Be available to assist and answer questions.

Other Considerations

- Secure a couple sound systems for practice time.

- Decide whether the tryouts are closed or open to the public.

- Arrange for someone to videotape tryout day for documentation.

- Decide if candidates will be trying out in groups or individually. If grouped, determine the number per group before tryouts so the students know. Decide if they can pick their group or if you will pick the group.

- Decide if you will do interviews.

- Find judges and decide how much you will pay them. Be sure to complete the proper paperwork from your school bookkeeper in order to have the checks ready for your judges.

- Obtain needed supplies, e.g. table for judges, pencils, pens, tabulation page, list of all candidates in order of performance, score sheets.

Coach's Evaluation

Name	Attendance (15points)	Packet (15 Points)	Poster (15 points)	Attitude (20 points)	Jumps (5 points)	Motions (5 points)	Questions (10 points)	Total (75 points)

Figure 4-11

Scoring and Evaluations

Set your criteria for judging. Scoring is often divided into different categories and percentages depending on your needs. For example: 40 percent performance score, 20 percent teacher evaluations, 20 percent interview, and 20 percent participation and attitude. Design your score sheet to reflect the needs of your program.

Means of Notification

You can notify candidates of the tryout results in many ways, including the following:

• Post the new squad list.

• Give everyone a sealed envelope with a letter thanking her for participating. In this note, write either "Congratulations, you made the squad…" or "Sorry, you did not make the squad." Have the senior cheerleaders pass these out after school. Since the seniors do not know what is in each envelope, they will treat everyone the same.

• Call each candidate personally.

• Announce the new cheer squad over the school PA system.

Tryouts take a lot of preparation and patience. When dealing with teenagers, you must be concerned with their self-image. Please be open-minded. Fill the cheer slots with students that would be the best representatives for your cheerleading program. Remember that athletes come in all sizes and they all have something different and wonderful to offer your squad. Choose wisely.

5

Teamwork and Motivation

"The power of messages often comes in a few well-chosen words. Words initiate thoughts. Thoughts provide motivation. Motivation produces action. A few words can speak volumes. Words coming from the right person, at the right moment, can go directly to the heart."

—Bruce Eamon Brown

You have selected a talented squad, met with the parents, and spent countless hours planning the season. Now, you must motivate the cheerleaders to work together in harmony as a team. Realize that teamwork is a continuous process and you are the catalyst to making it happen. You will be molding, forming, and developing responsible young adults. What you say and do affects not only how they work together but also how they perceive themselves.

A blueprint to building a successful team that works together for the common good includes the following:

• Clear communication

• Teamwork

• Teambuilding

• Motivation

Clear Communication

Both the coach and the cheerleaders must learn to send, receive, and respond to messages effectively. For the first few practices, everyone is excited about being a part of the cheerleading team, but at the same time, they are apprehensive to see where they fit in. Explain to them that the beginning stage is the forming, learning, and finding out where they belong

phase. They need to be willing to try different positions and new challenges. Showing them that you understand their feelings helps them cope with their insecurities.

After a few weeks, the newness wears off and people start to express their wants. Conflicts will happen. Teach the cheerleaders clear communication skills in order to work through the conflicts. In this stage, personalities start to show, for example, the leader, the negotiator, the manipulator, and the pacifist. Teach them all to turn conflict into opportunities for personal development and teamwork.

Steps to Work Through a Conflict

• Identify and state the problem/conflict.

• Express concerns/feelings with "I" statements not "you" statements.

• Listen to understand—never to interrupt.

• Check that you understand by briefly repeating what you heard in your own words.

• It is okay to laugh with each other but not at each other.

• Final resolution is achieved when one or more of the following takes place:

Apologies are exchanged.

Reconciliation occurs.

Everyone reaches a solution that they can "work with."

The solution allows the group to proceed.

Conflict Resolution Game: Reflective Listening

Have squad members listen to the feelings of one person and then reflectively paraphrase that person's feelings. The person whose feelings are paraphrased then responds to the accuracy of the reflective listeners.

Teamwork

Teamwork is a combination of cooperation, solidarity, collaboration, and working together. A strong cheer squad becomes one in purpose and desire. To create this synergy, use the following plan:

- Make everyone feel that she is an essential part of the team. Emphasize the importance of every position.

- Everyone has to have the same team goals. At the beginning of your season, have the group develop team goals. Post them on the wall for everyone to review every day. The goals must answer the following questions:

  What does the team stand for?

  What does the team want to accomplish?

- Everyone must commit to making these goals come true, and decide the following:

  How are we going to accomplish the goals as a team?

  What is the plan of action?

  What is every individual going to do to contribute to fulfilling our goals?

- The coach must encourage and support the team's effort. Develop athletes that know they

have control of their behaviors and reward their efforts. Develop values of leadership, courage, persistence, and commitment. Encourage, motivate, and reward their principles.

Teambuilding

Teambuilding games are a fun way to develop cohesiveness. They tear down walls in communications, provide avenues that encourage discussion, and increase productivity. Teambuilding takes time but the end results are well worth the effort. It is an ongoing process that boosts commitment. Do the following exercises with your squad to build a unified group.

To Be or Knot To Be—Everyone stands in a circle and reaches in with their right hand. With their left hand they grab the right hand that is in front of them. No one can hold both hands of one person. The squad then works together to untangle the knot without letting go of hands.

Ball of String—While standing in a circle, the team passes a ball of yarn from one person to another. The coach asks a question and only the person with the ball of yarn can talk. She then passes it to another cheerleader anywhere in the circle, while still holding onto the string. This process continues until everyone has had a turn. After everyone has answered the question, you will have a web of string. This web illustrates the interconnected nature of the group, showing the cheerleaders that everything they do and say at practice affects the entire group. Now show how they can work together by placing a balloon into the center of the web and having them keep the balloon from touching the floor. This game demonstrates teamwork.

School Spirit Sculpture—Give your squad different supplies, such as newspaper, scissors, construction paper, glitter, straws, tape, string, etc. and tell them to create a sculpture that represents their school's spirit. Have them explain the significance. If the school's spirit is low, use this opportunity to discuss how they can improve their school's spirit.

Trust Fall—Cheerleaders sit in a close circle with their legs straight and arms out. One cheerleader stands in the center of the circle. She should have everyone's feet around her ankles. The girl in the middle squeezes all her muscles and is very tight. She falls to the side and the other cheerleaders catch her and push her back and forth in the circle. Let all members have a turn in the center.

Cheerleader Tic-Tac-Toe—Set up nine chairs in three rows. Divide the squad into X's and O's. Just like in regular tic-tac-toe, the X's and O's alternate, except they sit in the chairs instead of writing on paper. Ask questions about the rules of football, basketball, or any sport. The cheerleaders must raise their hands to answer. If they are right, then they sit in one of the chairs. The first team to get three in a row (diagonally, vertically, or horizontally) wins.

Rock-Paper-Scissors Tag—Form two groups. During each turn, a team must decide whether they are *rock, paper*, or *scissors*. The teams face each other, and on the count of three everyone shows either rock, paper, or scissors. The team who wins chases the other team. If a chased team member gets caught before she reaches a designated home base, she becomes part of the other team.

Pass the Body—Cheerleaders lie on their backs on the floor. Their heads are lined up ear to ear in a straight line. Every other person extends her legs out to the opposite side. For example, when looking at the line, the first person extends her legs out to the left side of the line of heads, and the second person extends her legs to the right side. Repeat the pattern. Next, all the people on the floor extend their arms upward to the ceiling. Another person lies on her back on the hands of the cheerleaders on the floor. The top person has the tip of her head facing down the line of hands. This person must stay tight as a board. The object of the game is to move the top person down the row of hands without dropping her.

Motivation

Maintaining a team's enthusiasm is one of your top priorities. You must motivate them both extrinsically and intrinsically. Extrinsic motivation is from the outside: the coach, parents, and teammates. Do you reward positive behavior? To find out, ask yourself the following questions:

- Do you have a demerit system to maintain discipline?

- At games or practices, do you concentrate primarily on correcting their mistakes?

- Do you feel you spend more time disciplining your cheerleaders than anything else?

- Do you expend most of your energy on the few problem cheerleaders versus the rest of the team?

Often, coaches concentrate on what athletes do wrong and spend little time on reinforcing the positive accomplishments. Although your job is to teach the cheerleaders how to do things correctly, remember that it takes a special person to be a cheerleader and, as the coach, you must strengthen that concept of importance. Cheerleaders are the primary motivators of the school and you must be their motivator to sustain their enthusiasm. Instead of focusing on the negative, do the following:

- Concentrate on the good things that the cheerleaders do.

- Reward them individually and as a team every day.

- Redirect a negative behavior instead of simply reprimanding the behavior. Immediately recognize any change that leads to a positive behavior. Example: A cheerleader is always talking while in chant lines at the game. Tell her that you know she has lots of energy and sometimes that causes her to get a little chatty during the game. Ask her to focus that energy on shouting encouragements to the team. Finish the statement by confirming your confidence in her ability. Next "catch" her, as soon as you can, doing what you asked her and reconfirm that is what you wanted.

- Praise progress.

- Sandwich a change that you want with two positive statements.

- Make cheerleaders feel as though they are the most important people you know.

Some ways to apply these concepts to cheerleading include the following:

- Post a motivation quote of the day or week.

- Distribute motivational poems and articles to the team.

- Show motivational movies.

- Invite a college cheerleader to your practice to speak.

- Display charts where you can recognize accomplishments for jumps, stunts, learning all chants, etc.

- Post goals and check them off when achieved.

- Give a tangible reward. It does not have to be big or expensive. It is a symbol that shows them that you recognize what they have done and that they are important. Some examples of rewards include the following:

    Paper hand cutout with the words "High 5 for a job well done!" written on it.

    Personal note that says "Thank You for Going Above and Beyond." Have a picture of a cheerleader being basket-tossed on it.

    Stuffed frog with a tag around his neck that says "Best Jumper." Every game, the winner takes home the frog until the next game, when she will return the frog to the coach. The cheerleader takes the tag from the frog's neck and places it on her cheer bag. At the end of the season, reward the person who has the most tags.

    100% Shirt. At the end of practice, give out a special shirt that says "100%" to the cheerleader who gave 100%. She wears it until the next practice, then signs and returns it. Repeat at each practice.

- Start every practice by talking about what they've done right, be it last night's game or the last practice. Be careful not to say "You did great last night but you need to not talk so much while in your chant lines." They will only remember, "Don't talk in the chant line." You lost the positive statement by ending the compliment with a negative.

- Catch them doing things right and praise, praise, praise.

- Have a "Wall of Fame" and highlight the skills that the cheerleaders accomplished.

- Make a website about the cheerleaders.

- Feature a cheerleader of the week on the website.

- Have the cheerleaders practice outside in front of the school so others can see how hard they work.

- Send in articles and photos to local newspapers and the school paper about their accomplishments.

- Set a rule that "You can only complain if you have a solution to the problem." This guideline will help the cheerleaders learn how to resolve their own problems.

- Make special treats with motivational sayings attached to them.

- Explain to the cheerleaders the values they are learning from the work they are doing.

- Ask cheerleaders to conduct themselves responsibly by showing respect, courtesy, kindness, encouragement, humility, good sportsmanship, and a positive attitude. You are their role model. If you want them to display these values, you need to demonstrate these same values towards them.

- Verbally tell them about your beliefs in their abilities. Encourage often. Praise often.

Unity Games and Exercises

Unity games are fun activities that bond the team together and help them to understand the importance of principles and values, and, in turn, develop intrinsic motivation.

- Start and finish every practice, game, and competition with a team saying, slogan, or motto. The cheerleaders form a tight-knit circle with their right hands overlapped in the middle. Together they yell this saying. This daily gesture signals a bond of one unified group committed to a team goal.

- Everyone signs a commitment pledge to the team (Figure 5-1).

- Make a scrapbook of the season to illustrate the team's work and accomplishments. Delegate each person to do a section of the book.

- Take turns hosting a pre-game dinner at each other's houses. Make it a potluck. A team that plays together has a better understanding of each individual's personality.

- Have a big celebration banquet at the end of the year or season (see Chapter 12).

- At the end-of-the-year banquet, give a "letter of promise" to the graduating seniors (Figure 5-2). This letter acknowledges the leadership of the seniors and reinforces that they have left a legacy of hard work and success that will be carried into the future.

- Have an Easter party in September for a change of pace. Hide plastic Easter eggs around your practice area. Put small treats and quotes inside the eggs.

- Set up mailboxes for the cheerleaders where they leave appreciation notes to each other.

- At Thanksgiving, have everyone write personal thank you notes to each other.

Athletics teach valuable life skills. It is up to you to provide the means and opportunities for learning in both practices and game situations. What you teach your cheerleaders now will influence how they react and live in their adult lives.

Commitment Pledge

I pledge with all my heart to give my best to _____ during _____ because I am a significant contributor of a national-class, championship team. To show how serious I am, I commit to:

1. _____
_____
_____

2. _____
_____
_____

3. _____
_____
_____

4. _____
_____
_____

I accept my role on this team and will fulfill it.

_____   _____
Signature   Date

Figure 5-1

Letter of Promise

Dear _____,

We write you this letter to let you know that you will be greatly missed. We'll miss your determination, commitment, and supportive team attitude! As you move on to bigger and greater things in life, remember and feel proud that you have been a key part of the finest cheerleading squad in _____!

We, as underclassmen and coaches, make this oath to you. We promise the following. We will:

- Always have school spirit.
- Smile (even when we are losing).
- Display good sportsmanship.
- Rally at the end of every cheer.
- Support our school, our community, and our fellow cheerleaders.
- Remember our basics:
    - Dip and follow through.
    - Stay locked.
    - Stretch every day.
    - Work daily on jumps.
- Always believe in ourselves.
- Always make this team the best cheerleading squad in the state.

Why, you might ask, do we make this promise? So that when you come back later in life, you can say, I was part of this team, the best team in _____! We want you to be proud of the _____ cheerleaders now and in the future! You are and always will be a _____ cheerleader!

Your team, friends, and coaches,

Figure 5-2

6

Planning a Practice

"The lesson you teach today is not confined to the walls of your classroom. Once it is implanted in the heart and mind of a child, it can change the world."

—Unknown

Great coaches must teach, guide, inspire, and motivate. In order to do all of these tasks, you need to have a daily plan that incorporates all these fundamentals. Cheerleaders work not only on physical skills but leadership jobs and duties. Because of these many responsibilities, organization is vital to a successful cheer program. As the coach, you should write a list of activities and tasks for each month. Make an outline of what is needed for each of those tasks. Create calendars of all events, games, and practices. Distribute copies of calendars and lists of jobs to every cheerleader. Require each cheerleader to have a notebook in which to keep all handouts. Instruct them to bring that notebook to all practices. As the coach, you need to be prepared each day of practice with a detailed plan of the day or practice schedule. At the end of practice, have every cheerleader sign the back of this plan. This signed document provides you with a written confirmation of when you taught skills and who was there. Remember that by being organized, you are teaching this needed skill to your cheerleaders.

General Practice Outline

An effective practice contains the following components:

• Squad meeting

• Warm-up

• Conditioning and strength training

• Stretching

• Drills

• Chant/cheer review

• Dances

• Upcoming game plan

• Leadership tasks

• Team bonding

• Wrap-up and review

• Theme of the week

The amount of time distributed among these components will change depending on the activities and tasks that need to be accomplished in a particular week. A helpful hint is to post the outline for practice that day on the wall. Having a visual reminder helps keep everyone on task (see Figures 6-1 and 6-2).

Meeting

Start off practice with a 15-minute overview of what needs to be accomplished. Detail the timeline for each part of practice. You can also use this meeting time to do the following:

- Evaluate past game plans.

- Review and critique films from a game or competition.

- Open the floor for suggestions.

- Discuss the value of the week and how it applies to cheerleading.

Warm-up

Cheerleaders need to elevate their body temperature to promote blood flow and prepare the body to work. Warming up allows the muscles to contract and relax more efficiently, thereby helping to reduce injuries and soreness. During warm-up, it is also important to work the range of motion through the joints. Use any movement that involves large muscles, for example:

- Light jog

- Knee lifts

- Jumping rope

- Arm swings

- Body isolations

- Five minutes of chant movements

- Light aerobic dance moves

- Short band dances

Conditioning

Athletes must engage in a special and continuous conditioning program to prepare and maintain a high level of fitness. These general calisthenics include a variety of exercises that develop coordination, improve body awareness and alignment, strengthen muscles, increase metabolism, and strengthen the hearts and lungs. In the beginning of the season, delegate a couple cheerleaders as "conditioning trainers" to lead the team through a combination of conditioning and strengthening exercises specific to cheerleading. Do these exercises without a break to create an aerobic workout. Try to elevate the heart rate

to 60 to 70 percent of their maximum heart rate. (To calculate the heart rate goal, subtract the person's age from 220, then multiply by 0.6 or 0.7.) Exercise for 20 minutes in this range to get an aerobic training effect. Examples of conditioning exercises include the following:

- Heel raises

- Jumping jacks

- Lunges across the floor

- Plyometrics—switch lunges, one-legged hops in place, two-footed hops across the floor, squat jumps, scissor jumps, tuck jumps

- Plies or knee bends

- Kicks

- Down and outs—Squat to the floor, extend legs out, squat, stand.

- Chassés across the floor

- Push-ups

- V-up sit-ups

- Seated straddle lifts—The cheerleaders sit on the floor, keeping the back straight. They lift one leg up and down, keeping the leg straight. Repeat with other leg, then try both legs at the same time.

- Hollow rocks—The cheerleaders lay on the floor. They lift their legs and torsos by hollowing in the midsection. They rock back and forth.

- Sitting toe touches—The cheerleaders sit on the floor with their knees bent. They must balance so their feet barely touch the floor. Maintaining this position, they shoot their legs out to toe touch position, then return back to the original position.

Mix up the exercise routine to prevent boredom or overuse syndrome. Other options are exercise videos, kickboxing, Pilates, and circuit training (Figure 6-3). Another variation is using bonding games like wheelbarrow races, blanket pull, tug of war, and scooter races to develop needed physical skills.

Practice Plan

3:00   Meeting

_____

_____
_____

3:15   Warm-up

_____

_____
_____

3:30   Conditioning

_____

_____
_____

3:45   Drills

_____

_____
_____

4:15   Chant/cheer review

_____

_____
_____

4:30   Team bonding game

_____

4:45   Leadership tasks

_____

_____
_____

5:15   Wrap-up and review

_____

_____
_____

Figure 6-1

Competitive Team Practice

3:00   Meeting

_____
_____
_____

3:15   Warm-up

_____
_____
_____

3:30   Conditioning

_____
_____
_____

3:45   Drills (tumbling)

_____
_____
_____

4:15   Team bonding game

_____

4:30   Competition routine

_____
_____
_____

5:20   Wrap-up and review

_____
_____
_____

Figure 6-2

Circuit Training

Set up the following 10 stations in a circle:

1. Two five-pound free weights
2. Jump rope
3. Stretch bands
4. Jumping jacks
5. Squats
6. Jog
7. Push-ups
8. Tuck jumps
9. Sit-ups
10. Kicks

Each cheerleader starts at one of the stations, spends two minutes performing the exercise, then rotates to the station to her right. She continues this process until she has completed all 10 drills.

Figure 6-3

Strength Training

Have your athletic trainer set up a weight-training program for your cheerleaders. The benefits of strength training are muscle strength and endurance, and muscle tone. Strength training also contributes to efficiency in athletic performance and decreases the likelihood of injuries. Rules for strength training include the following:

- Work muscles from largest to smallest.

- Work lower back/buttock, legs, torso, arms, shoulders, abdominals.

- Work both sides of the muscle.

- Work full range of motion.

- Decide how many repetitions and sets of repetitions to do.

- Decide how much weight to lift.

- Set the amount of rest time between repetitions (usually two to four seconds) and amount of time between sets (usually one to two minutes).

- Do not work the same muscle group every day. Muscles need a day to repair.

- Always use a spotter when lifting heavy weights.

Stretching

Cheerleaders need to stretch to develop flexibility, which in turn prevents pulling muscles while performing jumps, splits, kicks, dances, and cheer motions. Flexibility refers to the range of motion possible at a joint. Stretching is the process used to lengthen the muscles and connective tissues. Three types of stretching are static, ballistic, and dynamic. Static stretching means holding the joint in a locked position and stretching the muscles and tendons to the greatest range possible for 20 to 30 seconds. An example of static stretching is splits. Ballistic stretching involves bouncing movements at the end of the range of motion. Be careful when using this method because the risk of injury is higher. Dynamic stretching involves using a range of motion in the joint during the performance of an activity.

Stretching should be a part of every practice to prepare the muscles for movement, maintain flexibility, develop body awareness, reduce muscle soreness, and improve personal performance. These athletes need to stretch gradually and regularly, using proper technique to avoid injury. Tailor your routine to the needed areas of stretching.

PNF (proprioceptive neuromuscular facilitation) is a technique that helps increase range of motion. Using two people, one person gently assists the other's stretch by lengthening the muscle and holding it in that position for 20 to 30 seconds. The stretcher relaxes and then repeats the same movement, with the partner stretching the muscle a little further.

The entire body can be stretched in 15 minutes of practice time. Start with the feet and work your way up the body. Have your cheerleaders perform the following progression of stretches:

- Ankle/foot—Standing on one foot, put body weight slightly on the opposite toe and roll the foot around in circles. Repeat with the other foot.

- Lower leg—Place the ball of the foot against the wall and lean into the wall while stretching the calves. Do on both legs.

- Hamstrings—Stand against a wall facing a partner. The partner lifts the leg as high as possible (keeping the leg straight) and holds for 30 seconds. Repeat on opposite leg.

- Adductors—Lie on the floor with legs in a diamond position (feet together and knees bent). A partner pushes the legs toward the floor and holds for 30 seconds.

- Quadriceps—Standing, hold onto the wall. Bend the knee and grab the foot behind with the opposite hand. Pull the foot towards the buttock and hold for 30 seconds. Repeat with opposite leg.

- Hips—Lie on the stomach on the floor. Reach behind and grab the ankles. Pull upward, arching back slightly, and hold for 30 seconds.

- Lower torso—Face away from the wall. Lean back and place hands on the wall and walk the hands down the wall. Have a partner spot this exercise.

- Upper back—Face the wall, standing arm's length away. With feet apart, bend at the waist and touch the wall. Keeping the arms straight, lean into the wall. Hold. The body should be bent at a 90-degree angle.

- Arms—With the elbow bent, raise one arm overhead next to the ear and reach with the hand for the opposite shoulder blade. Grab the elbow with the opposite hand and pull it behind the head. Hold for 30 seconds. Repeat with the other arm.

- Wrists—On all fours, place hands on the floor with fingertips turned towards the knees. Lean back slightly and hold for 30 seconds.

- Chest—Sitting or standing, reach both arms behind the back. Keeping the arms as straight as possible, grab the hands and pull outward, away from the body. Hold.

- Shoulders—Raise one arm to shoulder level, and bend the elbow. With the opposite hand, grab the elbow and push towards the body. Hold.

- Neck—Tilt the head towards the shoulder. Reach across the head and gently pull towards the shoulder and hold. Do in both directions.

Drills

Use drills to develop proficiency in required skills such as jumping, tumbling, stunting, and motion technique. See Chapter 7 for examples of drills for each area.

Chant and Cheer Review

For sideline cheerleading, chants and cheers are the heart of your program. They are the elements that motivate the crowd to yell during a fast-paced basketball game or when the football team is about to score from the three-yard line.

Review last year's list of chants. Keep the traditional ones that the crowd always responds to, delete the older chants, and add new ones. Let the cheerleaders make up the words and moves for new ones. They will surprise you with their creativity and will also enjoy performing them at games because of their pride and ownership in them. Don't forget to review the free-form chants that get your audience on their feet stomping or using hand motions.

Use the chant review as a warm-up activity to accomplish two things at one time. While rehearsing the chants and cheers, remind the cheerleaders to practice as if they were in front of an audience, concentrating on sharp arm movements, loud voices, and big smiles on their faces. The more they do these things, the more natural cheerleading becomes to them and the better they can concentrate on tuning into the audience's needs.

Dances

Ask your band director to make a copy of all the band music so dances can be choreographed. Dance routines are another opportunity to have your cheerleaders be creative by letting them do the choreography. In the beginning of the season, use this choreographing time as a team bonding game. Divide the team into groups of three or four. Each group choreographs a dance, and then teaches it to the rest of the squad. If the team is learning a longer dance to perform at halftime or an assembly, teach small sections of it each day. The mind needs time to absorb the details of a move and by teaching a routine in smaller increments, you will be able to get better precision and synchronizations from your cheerleaders. Remember, you can use your band dances as your warm-up section. It sets an upbeat mood to the start of practice.

Upcoming Game Plan

The following elements should be in your game plan:

- Time and place to meet

- What uniform to where

- Warm-up schedule

- List of chants and who calls them

- Stunts that can be used with chants

- Chants that use signs and spirit items

- Formation for cheerleaders to line up on the sidelines

- Coordinator for signs, banners, and any other spirit items

- When to line up for the start of the game

- Where to line up for the National Anthem

- When to be on the field for run-through banner at halftime

- When to meet and greet opponent's cheerleaders

- Whether or not you will supply cheerleaders with food and drinks, and who will be in charge of providing them

- Who will clean up at the end of the game, put away the signs, banners, and spirit items

- What to do if the crowd becomes unruly

- Where the administrators and security are, if needed

- Expectations of cheerleaders at games (The coach should do a game evaluation. See Chapter 10.)

Review all these details ahead of time at practice and then again at the game. Often, the cheerleaders will have to adapt to quick changes resulting from the different facilities, a missing cheerleader due to unforeseen circumstances, changes in weather, and the mood of the crowd. Reviewing your game plan at practice will help them to be better cheerleaders and will also help them adapt to needed changes.

Leadership Tasks

Depending on the season and time of year, these responsibilities will vary. Set aside 15 to 30 minutes during each practice to work on the assignments you gave each cheerleader during pre-season planning (see Chapter 2). Split the cheerleaders into groups in order to accomplish more tasks in a shorter timeframe. Remember to encourage cheerleaders to write an outline of the job and a time for completion. Have them keep everything in their cheer notebook.

Team Bonding Games

Because of the intensity of practice, it is a good idea to break it up with short games that add an element of fun and help bond the team together. Following are a few effective examples:

- *Two Truths and a Lie*—Every person writes three sentences: two truths and one lie about herself. The coach will read the three statements and the team guesses who wrote them. Once they guess the person, then they need to determine which statement is the lie.

- *Scavenger Hunt*—Divide the group into two teams and give each group a list of items to find. The first team to collect all the items wins.

- *Team on the Towel*—The team tries to get everyone on a towel within a time limit. Split the team into two and have them compete against each other.

- *Monster Race*—Divide the group into two smaller teams. Each group must create a monster by attaching their bodies together. The monster must make a sound and move from one place to another with only a certain number of feet and hands on the ground. Both groups have five minutes to complete the task and cross the finish line.

- *Pass the Hula Hoop*—The cheerleaders join hands and form a circle. One person has a hula hoop around her arm. The object is to pass the hoop around the circle without breaking the chain.

- *Build a Machine*—Divide the cheerleaders into several groups. Each group builds a machine (e.g., washing machine, toaster, computer, vacuum cleaner, dishwasher) with only their bodies. After 10 minutes, each group shows the machine and the other teams guess what it is.

- *Three Things About the Squad*—As the squad sits in a circle, each cheerleader responds to three questions determined by the coach. Only one person speaks at a time. Questions could include the following:

    What is one positive thing about the team?

    What is something that you would like to change about the squad?

    What is something new that you would like the squad to try?

Spending time on these bonding games rejuvenates your squad and brings them closer together. See Chapter 5 for more ideas on how to motivate your cheerleaders.

Wrap Up and Review

At the end of every practice, do a quick overview that includes the following activities:

- Have cheerleaders sign the practice schedule.

- Briefly detail the accomplishments of practice.

- Remind cheerleaders of upcoming deadlines for assigned tasks.

- Hand out needed paperwork.

- Review the "value of the week."

- Thank them for all their hard work and commitment.

- End with a team motto or saying.

Theme of the Week

All of the components discussed in this chapter are needed for a well-run program, but a coach should also build character and self-esteem. A fun and educational way to develop these traits is to have a theme of the week. For example, each week, display a word of value: commitment, honesty, follow-through, teamwork, respect, or sportsmanship. Post the word and its definition. At the beginning of practice, talk about the word, its importance, and its application to cheerleading. Throughout practice, emphasize the theme or word of the week. Use the word often while coaching. At the end of practice, during the wrap-up session, tell the cheerleaders how they applied that value to practice.

7

Skills and Drills

"The eight laws of learning are explanation, demonstration, imitation, repetition, repetition, repetition, repetition, and repetition."

—John Wooden

The basic skills for cheerleading are jumping, stunting, tumbling, and motions. To master these skills, teams must do exercises. Develop drills for cheerleading by breaking down the different components of each required skill. These exercises need to work both strength and flexibility.

Jumps

Types of Jumps

* *Tuck (Figure 7-1)*—Legs are lifted in front of the body and knees are bent. Arms are in a high V position.

* *Star or Spread Eagle (Figure 7-2)*—Legs are lifted to the side with knees locked and turned forward. Arms are in a high V.

* *Right and Left Hurdler (Figures 7-3a and 7-3b)*—Depending on the jump, one leg is extended parallel to the floor (or higher) and the other leg is bent toward the back as it is pulled up in the air. Both arms are extended straight out in a T position.

* *Right and Left Front Hurdler (Figures 7-4a and 7-4b)*—Cheerleader faces diagonally to the front. Depending on the jump, one leg is lifted as high as possible and straight toward the body. The other leg is bent with the knee pointing toward the floor.

Figure 7-1

Figure 7-2

- *Herkie*—The jump is similar to a side hurdler except the arm of the bent leg is bent to the waist and the straight leg arm is also straight. Lawrence Herkimer, founder of the National Cheerleaders Association, created this jump.

- *Toe Touch (Figure 7-5)*—Legs are lifted straight to the side as high as possible with hips and knees rotated out. The arms are in a T position.

- *Pike (Figure 7-6)*—Cheerleaders stand diagonally to the front. Straight legs are lifted together as high as possible and the arms are straight and together as the cheerleader pikes in the torso.

- *Double Nine (Figure 7-7)*—Legs are lifted in the air, forming a number nine position. The arms match the movement of the number nine.

- *Around the World*—This move is a combination jump of hitting a pike, then rotating the legs and arms to the side.

Figure 7-4a

Figure 7-4b

Figure 7-3a

Figure 7-5

Figure 7-3b

Figure 7-6

Figure 7-7

Four fundamentals to implementing perfect jumps are the approach, takeoff, execution, and landing. Cheerleaders must work each section in order to execute great jumps. Teaching the jump to counts helps cheerleaders to understand each part. The *approach* to the jump is a clasp of hands under the chin, feet together to count 1, 2, then arms hit a high V as the cheerleader raises upon her toes on count 3, 4. For the *takeoff*, arms circle inward on count 5 as she bends her knees and propels off the floor, executing the jump on count 6, and *lands* on the balls of her feet with her legs together, knees bent, and arms at her side on count 7, 8. This method is only one of several types of approaches.

Drills for Jumps

Jump Lines—Divide the group into lines of four or five people. Play upbeat music. The person in front of each line performs a specific jump synchronized with the music. Each jump is done to counts in order to understand every move needed for proper execution. After executing the jump, the cheerleader moves to the back of the line to her right. Repeat the drill until everyone performs the jump four times. Do the same drill with all the jumps. This drill is a fun way to perfect jumps because the music adds interest and energy to the learning process. As you evaluate the jumps, critique proper arm placements and body alignment, jump height, torso lift, and landing.

Assisted Partner Jumps—Two cheerleaders face each other. One cheerleader extends her hands, palms up, as the other cheerleader places her hands and arms in her partner's arms. The first cheerleader lifts the other cheerleader as she executes a jump. This drill allows the jumping cheerleader to work on technique such as body alignment and toe point. Repeat jump 10 times. Reverse positions and repeat sequence.

V-ups—The cheerleader lies on the floor. As she performs a sit-up, both arms and legs extend to the side in a straddle position.

Tuck Jumps—The cheerleader jumps up and down, pulling her knees up in front of the body. She should always land on the balls of the feet and absorb the impact through the legs. Perform 30 times. Tuck jumps are plyometric exercises that combine speed and strength to help develop the muscles in the legs. Stronger leg muscles lead to higher jumps.

Kicks—A person stands with her back against a wall. Keeping the back straight and against the wall, she kicks the leg as high as possible, keeping the leg straight and toes pointed. Make sure the supporting leg stays straight, too. Kick 30 times on each leg.

Hang Drill—The cheerleader hangs from a bar so that her legs are off the floor. She lifts her legs into a straddle position using her abdominal muscles. She must keep her legs straight and toes pointed. Do 10 times, relax, and repeat.

Leg Tosses—Cheerleaders pair off. One person lies on her back with her legs together in the air. The second person stands behind the head of the cheerleader on the floor and tosses her partner's legs downward. In turn, the cheerleader on the floor must tighten her abdominals and resist the movement.

Partner Stretching—One person lies on the floor with the torso bent at the waist and the legs in a straddle position. The partner kneels on the floor facing that person and places her hands on the person's thighs and applies gentle pressure downward. Hold that position for a count of 30. Relax and repeat the drill again.

Stunting

Stunting is elevating a partner in the air. Depending on the composition of your squad, stunts can be done with two people (mostly with co-ed teams) or with three to four people if you have an all-girl squad. Basic stunts are explained in Chapter 8. To perform these stunts, cheerleaders need to work on strength and rhythm for both the base (the person holding the stunt in the air) and the flyer (the person who is extended in the air).

Drills for Stunting

Spotting drills are the key to safety in cheerleading. Spotting is probably the most difficult element for cheerleaders to learn. When a person is falling towards them, instinct tells them to protect themselves first; therefore, they move away from the falling person. Spotting is a learned activity. You should never assume that just because you, as their coach, tell the cheerleaders to catch the falling person, they automatically will do it.

Ground Level Spotting Drill—Divide team into stunt groups: two side people, back spotter, and flyer. Flyer stands, with her arms at her side, in front of the two side bases and the back spotter. The two bases and the back spotter bend at the knees and catch the flyer as she falls back into their arms. Progress to the next level and now the flyer will jump backward into their arms.

Step Off Bench Spotting Drill—Flyer stands, with her arms over her head and hands clasped together, on a bench or bottom row of a bleacher. Two bases stand on either side of the flyer. As the flyer dismounts, the spotters reach up to the flyer and catch her in a tight hug position, pulling the flyer close to their bodies and lifting the flyer upward and resisting during the catch (Figure 7-8). This technique is called the "bear hug." Flyer must keep her body tight and arms up at all times.

Figure 7-8

Hanging Drill for Flyer—Two cheerleaders face each other as the flyer grabs the shoulders of the cheerleaders and hangs with her legs tucked up to her chest. This drill is similar to loading in for a stunt, but the flyer holds her own body weight in her arms (Figure 7-9).

Figure 7-9

Weighted Ball Drill—Bases practice stunt techniques with a weighted ball substituted for the flyer. Synchronize timing for both getting into the stunt and elevating it in the air.

Plies—Use this drill to teach the proper technique of a plie or knee bend. Knees must remain directly over the toes and should be at a 90-degree angle. Chest stays up and derriere is tucked in. Do this drill 20 times.

Stunt Plies for Bases—Two people base a flyer in a shoulder-level stunt and bend their knees no lower than 90 degrees. They bend then straighten 10 times. Be sure to have a back spotter to assist in keeping the stunt safe. Bases need to keep their backs straight and their knees aligned over the toes. Flyer needs to stay tight.

Balance Drill for Flyer—Flyer steps up onto a bench and locks the supporting leg as she balances her body weight on that one leg. Always have the flyer looking forward and not down at her feet.

Tumbling

Tumbling involves gymnastic elements such as standing back handspring, front handspring, roundoff back handspring, tuck, and full twist. The foundation to these elements is strength in both the arm/shoulder area and the legs. Key building blocks include the following:

- Handstand—Hands on the floor with legs elevated above the body in a straight line over the head. Everything stays aligned and head remains between the shoulders.

- Forward Roll—Squat to the floor, then body rolls forward with head tucked into the chest.

- Handstand Forward Roll—Initiate the handstand, then forward roll out of it.

- Cartwheel—A sideward wheel-type movement where one hand, then the other, touches the floor as the legs follow over the head.

- Back Walkovers—A back bend followed by the legs kicking over the head one at a time.

- Back Limber—Similar to a back walkover except both legs go over the head at the same time.

- Roundoffs—Step, hop, or hurdle, then both hands touch the floor as the legs snap over the body. As the legs touch the floor, the hands come off the ground.

Spotting is needed while learning these fundamentals. A spotter must have complete understanding of the mechanics of tumbling skills. She should also have the strength to support the weight of the tumbler. A cheerleader must perform the listed skills consistently with good form and execution before working back handsprings and other advanced tumbling skills.

Drills for Tumbling

Handstand Pop—Hit a handstand and immediately shrug the shoulders and pop back to the feet.

Wall Shoulder Shrugs—Face the wall. Extend arms straight out from the chest. Lean into the wall and immediately pop off the wall by shrugging the shoulders. Perform 30 times.

Walking Handstands—Hit a handstand. Walk across the floor on the hands.

Wall Sits—Sit with the back against the wall and knees bent. Hold that position for 30 seconds. Repeat drill.

Back Arches—Also known as bridges or back bends. Lay on the back on the floor. Arch the back, lifting the body into the air and supporting it only with the hands and feet.

Motions

Arms

Cheerleaders perform cheers and chants using strong, sharp arm motions. Every arm move must snap from one position to another. Each motion has a name.

- *T Motion (Figure 7-10)*—Arms extended out to the side parallel to the floor

Figure 7-10

- *Broken T (Figure 7-11)*—Arms bent at the elbow in front of the chest. Hands in a fist.

Figure 7-11

- *L Motion (Figure 7-12)*—One arm extended straight up beside the head and the other arm extended to the side, parallel to the floor. This motion can be done either to the right or the left.

Figure 7-12

- *Touchdown (Figure 7-13)*—Both arms extended straight up and close to the head.

Figure 7-13

- *Low Touchdown (Figure 7-14)*—Both arms extended straight down in front of the body.

Figure 7-14

- *High V (Figure 7-15)*—Arms extended up in a V position.

Figure 7-15

- *Low V (Figure 7-16)*—Both arms extended downward in an inverted V.

Figure 7-16

- *Daggers (Figure 7-17)*—Arms bent at the elbows, fists by the shoulders, and elbows tucked in close to the body.

Figure 7-17

- *Diagonal (Figure 7-18)*—One arm extended up diagonally and the other arm extended down diagonally. This motion can be done both right and left diagonal.

Figure 7-18

- *Bow and Arrow (Figure 7-19)*—One arm extended straight to the side, parallel to the floor, and the other arm bent at the elbow and also parallel to the floor.

Figure 7-19

- *Clasp (Figure 7-20)*—Both hands grasp together under the chin with elbows tucked into the body.

Figure 7-20

- *Clap (Figure 7-21)*—Hands come together with fingers straight.

Figure 7-21

- *Overhead Clasp (Figure 7-22)*—Arms extended overhead with hands clasped together.

Figure 7-22

- *K Motion (Figure 7-23)*—One arm extended down diagonal across the body. The other arm extended diagonally up and to the side.

Figure 7-23

- *Low Clasp (Figure 7-24)*—Arms extended downward in front of the body with hands clasped together.

Figure 7-24

- *Punch (Figure 7-25)*—One arm extended straight up with hand in a fist. The other hand on the hip.

Figure 7-25

Feet

The placement of the feet is just as important as the arms. The arm movements can be done with the feet apart, feet together, or in one of the following positions:

- *Side Lunge (Figure 7-26)*—One leg is extended to the side, the other leg is bent at the knee.

Figure 7-26

- *Back Lunge (Figure 7-27)*—One leg is extended to the back, the other leg is bent at the knee.

Figure 7-27

- *Double Lunge (Figure 7-28)*—Both knees are bent, with the hips and knees facing to the side. Torso is facing to the front.

Figure 7-28

- *Double Knee Bend (Figure 7-29)*—Also called a plie. Feet are apart and both knees are bent. Toes and feet are turned out.

Figure 7-29

Drills for Motions

"Coach Says"—This drill is a great way to improve skills and have fun at the same time. Coach yells out the name of a move. The cheerleaders will only perform that move when she shouts, "Coach says," and then adds the name of the movement. If a cheerleader does the move when the coach only says the move, then that cheerleader is out of the game. The last one left is the winner.

Hit It—Coach yells the name of the movement, then says "1, 2, 3, hit it." The cheerleaders execute the move with a snap on the words "hit it."

These drills will develop proper technique, needed strength, and flexibility for the cheerleaders. Adding them to your daily practices is key to developing well-skilled cheerleaders.

8

Stunting and Safety

"Spectacular achievements are always preceded by unspectacular preparation."

—Roger Staubach

Stunting is an integral part of cheerleading. Every coach's number one priority is the health and safety of their athletes. Remember that you are ultimately liable for your program. The best way to prevent injury to your cheerleaders is to learn as much as you can by attending clinics and seminars on stunting, safety, and liability. Check with your state coaches association, athletic director, and other coaches for information about clinics in your area. Take advantage of these resources to help advance your knowledge. Two outstanding safety certification organizations are the National Safety Council of Spirit Education and the American Association of Cheerleading Coaches and Advisors. By attending workshops and getting safety certifications, you are demonstrating your commitment to keeping your team safe.

Protecting your athletes also means properly planning activities and understanding your duty. You must provide a safe physical environment with proper equipment to reduce risk and prevent injury. Supervise all activities closely.

Assess your athletes' performance readiness. Know their fears and limitations. Know their medical history. Be sure that all cheerleaders have a current physical on file with your athletic office.

Know the rules for stunting. Each coach should have a copy of the National Federation of State High School Spirit Rules Book. It is updated yearly. This pamphlet contains information on definitions, general risk management, sportsmanship/conduct, dance/drill/pom safety, points of emphasis, regulations for coaches, regulations for participants, and guidelines for spirit competitions. All school-based coaches must follow these rules. All-star coaches do have some leeway on these regulations at national competitions, but coaches at the state level often are required to follow these same rules.

Because stunting is considered a "high risk" activity, a coach must distribute and post written rules on procedures and guidelines. Following is a list of recommended rules to post.

* Practice stunting area should be matted and free of obstructions.

* Ceiling needs to be high enough for stunts and tosses.

* All students must have a current physical on file and accident insurance coverage before participating in any element of cheerleading.

* All cheerleaders must complete an emergency treatment release form.

* Cheerleaders must wear proper clothing and shoes for the activity.

* Cheerleaders must be physically able to participate in the activity of the day. If ill or injured, they must notify the coach immediately.

- An emergency plan is posted on the cheer bulletin board with emergency phone number, facility phone number, and address with the name of the cross street.

- All cheerleaders must learn the rules and pass a written test before doing any stunting.

- No one can stunt unless the coach is present and carefully monitoring the building of stunts and pyramids.

- All cheerleaders will follow the stunt progression, starting with the basics and mastering each stunt before moving on to the more advanced levels. (Keep a written chart on each cheerleader. Both the coach and the cheerleader initial the chart when a stunt is successfully performed five times in a row.)

- Everyone must learn proper spotting technique before stunting.

- All cheerleaders will only perform legal stunts at practices, games, assemblies, performances, and competitions according to the National Federation of High School Spirit Rules.

- The coach needs to approve all stunts performed at games and other public activities.

- The cheering surface at games must be checked before performing perfected stunts to be sure it is dry, safe, and free of obstructions.

- These rules will be strictly enforced throughout the season. Failure to follow these rules will cause suspension of the cheerleader from the squad.

Risk Management

Cheerleading can be relatively safe and very rewarding with the proper procedures, safety rules, supervision, and equipment. Because cheerleading is physically demanding, you need to make athletes and parents aware of the inherent risks involved. Have both the cheerleader and parent sign a copy of the cheerleading safety guidelines (Figure 8-1). Keep written records of every meeting, practice, and injury.

Make sure you understand the following legal terms in order to meet your lawful obligations:

- *Legal Duty*—Your responsibility for the care and safety of others.

- *Reasonable Care*—Your degree of care is the same as a reasonable prudent person would exercise in the same situation.

- *Standard of Care*—The standard of care as agreed by the consensus of a group of reasonable people.

- *Negligence*—Failing to perform your legal duty.

- *Liability*—Negligence must lead to or cause injury in order for civil liability to be imposed.

You need to have CPR/first aid safety certification and renew it annually. Educate your cheerleaders on the proper procedure when an emergency happens. Post an emergency plan and keep an emergency kit that includes the following:

- Band-aids (multiple sizes)

- Prewrap

- Tape

- Hydrogen peroxide

- Petroleum jelly

- Hand disinfectant

- Compresses (multiple sizes)

- Triangle bandages or piece of cloth

- Scissors and tweezers

- Antiseptic wipes

- Bee sting kit

- Pencil and paper

- Spray bottle of 10% bleach solution

- Roll of gauze

- Ace wrap

- Non-stick pads

- Plastic bags

Cheerleading Safety Guidelines

This school strives to protect students from possible injury while engaging in school activities. Cheerleading is reasonably safe as long as certain guidelines are followed, but, like any athletic activity, it does have an inherent risk of injury. The guidelines and/or practices identified below have been established for this activity in order to protect the students and others from injury and/or illness. Participants and their parents/guardians should recognize that conditioning, nutrition, proper techniques, safety procedures, and well-fitting equipment are important aspects of this training program. Each participant is expected to follow the directions/standards of the coach.

Travel to and from off-campus facilities shall be in accordance with the directions of the coach.

Guidelines are as follows:

- Make certain that you wear all equipment that is issued by the coach. Advise the coach of any poorly fitted or defective equipment.

- Advise the coach if you are ill or have any prolonged symptoms of illness.

- Advise the coach if you are injured.

- Engage in warm-up exercises prior to participation in strenuous activity.

- Be alert for any physical hazards in the locker room or in and around the participation area. Advise the coach of any hazard.

- Practice and perfect stunts and tumbling prior to the event that you perform in.

- Follow National Federation Spirit Rules at all times.

- Lead cheers at appropriate times so you will be aware of the ball and of players' positioning to prevent possible injury.

- Be aware of the supervisory staff of both teams and where they can be located so they may be contacted in case of emergency or to offer assistance in controlling undesirable crowd behavior.

The above information has been explained to me and I understand the list of rules and procedures. I also understand the proper techniques required while participating in the cheerleader program.

_____   _____
Athlete's signature   Date

_____   _____
Parent's/Guardian's signature   Date

Figure 8-1

- Paper bags
- Latex gloves
- Tongue depressor
- Eyewash
- Nail clippers
- Safety pins
- Small sewing kit
- Chemical ice packs (or immediate access to ice)
- Splint material
- Tampons (also good for bloody noses)
- Cell phone
- Hard candy
- Highway flares
- Blanket
- Emergency plan
- Medical release forms for each cheerleader
- School accident form
- Accident report form (Figure 8-2)

Accident Report

General Information

District_____Date Completed _____

Name of District Contact Person _____

Name of Student Injured _____ Phone _____

Date of Injury _____ Time _____

Location _____

Description of Incident _____

_____

_____

_____

Witness _____Phone _____

Identify Agent Called to Scene (Police, Fire, etc.) _____

Name of Injured _____ Circle one: Student Employee Other

Address _____

Name of Parent _____

Home Phone _____ Work Phone _____

Extent of Injury _____

_____

_____

Name of Person in Charge _____ Title _____

Phone _____ Present at the Scene? Yes No

Action Taken by Person in Charge _____

_____

_____

_____

Figure 8-2

Your emergency plan should include the following:

- A designated person to call emergency services

- A person to stay with the injured cheerleader to administer reassurance

- Location of the nearest phone

- Phone number for emergency services

- Name, address, and cross street of the facility

- Location of emergency kit and forms

- Emergency plan of action (Figure 8-3)

- Specific meeting place in case of fire or other evacuation

When traveling, have a written passenger list. Keep one copy in the vehicle and leave one copy with a home administrator. For away games, meet with the other team's coach and familiarize yourself with their emergency plan.

Emergency Plan of Action

1. During an emergency, _____ will stay with the injured cheerleader. If the coach is the injured person, _____ will be assigned to stay with her.

2. The closest phone is located at _____.
Call 911 and give the dispatcher the following information:

- Address of school

- Nearest cross street

- Location of injured victim and a brief description of injury

Tell the dispatcher what first aid is being given. Tell the dispatcher that you have someone ready to direct the ambulance to where the injured victim is. Speak slowly. Stay on the phone until the dispatcher tells you to hang up.

3. Two people meet the ambulance and direct the medics to the correct location.

4. Coach calls parent or guardian.

5. If coach goes to the hospital with the injured cheerleader, practice is canceled for the day.

6. Return this sheet to the emergency kit.

IMPORTANT NUMBERS

High School _____   Coach _____

Athletic Director's Work Phone_____   Home Phone _____

Principal's Office Phone _____   Home Phone _____

Poison Control _____   Police _____

Hospital Emergency_____

Figure 8-3

When assessing an injury, follow these procedures:

- Remain calm and be very reassuring to the cheerleader.

- Ask the cheerleader her name to see if she is coherent.

- Ask if she feels dizzy or nauseous.

- Ask what happened.

- Ask where it hurts.

- Slide your hand over her body to check for any bleeding or obvious broken bones.

- Ask if the pain is sharp or dull. Does it move around or stay in one spot? Ask her to give details.

- Ask if this injury has occurred before.

- If it is a head, neck, or back injury, do not move the cheerleader. Call 911.

- If the cheerleader lost consciousness for more than 30 seconds or her pupils are unequal or unresponsive, call 911 immediately.

Hydration

It is absolutely necessary that athletes stay hydrated to prevent injury and to avoid heat illness and cramping. Basic rules for staying hydrated are the following:

- Drink 17 to 20 ounces two hours prior to exercise.

- Take water breaks every 15 minutes during practices and games. Athletes should drink 7 to 10 ounces of water at breaks.

- After practices and games, drink a minimum of 24 ounces of water.

- Consume sports drinks to promote fluid retention. Their carbohydrate electrolyte solution also provides fuel to the brain and muscles.

Evaluate and Classify Athletes

The coach should determine what position each cheerleader will perform in order to meet the needs of the team. Often, cheerleaders want to be a "flyer" or "front spot." They want to choose their friends to be part of their stunt team. As the coach, you should know what skills are needed in order to properly perform certain physical skills. Evaluate each athlete individually to match her strength and skills to the position that fits her abilities. Each athlete needs to have the power, strength, understanding, flexibility, and ability to adequately perform the skills for her position.

Stunt Progression

In stunt progression, a coach looks at two primary elements in relationship to cheerleaders: stunts and dismounts. Each element must be practiced and perfected at the lowest level before advancing to shoulder and overhead levels. Proper technique has to be developed for both the bases and flyers. Each component of a stunt and dismount should be broken down into its simplest elements.

- Cheerleaders need to learn in progression to understand the basics of stunting, starting with the easiest movements and advancing step by step through each level.

- Cheerleaders learn basic climbing techniques, body awareness, strength, and balance in order to perfect a stunt and maintain safety.

- Trust needs to be developed between the bases and flyer of each stunt group.

- Coaches need to evaluate and determine the proper ability level of each cheerleader and therefore set a standard of care. Every coach and cheerleader should use a stunt progression chart (see Figure 4-2 in Chapter 4).

Basic Rules for Stunting

- No one should talk while stunting except the coach or the third base (back spotter).

- While stunting, the third base (back spotter) calls out everything—the stunt that is being performed, when to start, when to break, when to cradle, etc.

- Every stunt should be done to a count so that everyone has the same timing.

- Everyone should know when to bend and when to lock.

- Everyone should know what position she has and what her job will be during the stunt. Each position is important. Be sure cheerleaders know that stunting is a team effort.

- Stunts should be smooth and controlled. Every person in the stunt should be working together in one synchronized movement. Timing is as important to proper stunting as strength.

Parts of a Stunt

Base (bottom person, primary, secondary)

- Base should know how to catch before attempting any stunting.

- Two bases should stand no further apart than the width of the flyer's shoulders.

- Base needs to control her hips in order to maintain stability and balance.

- Base bends her knees and distributes her weight evenly over the knees, ankles, and toes, and keeps her back straight.

- Base should not lean forward when the flyer loads into her hands.

- Base needs to know that the primary power is centered in her legs.

- Base starts with legs approximately shoulder-width apart. As the flyer loads into the hands of the bases, the power explodes from the legs first, through the shoulders, and up through the arms, which lock out at the top of the stunt. Legs and arms should lock out together at the top of the stunt.

- Base should not back up while stunting.

- Base should feel no weight in the transition from the load-in until the stunt hits the top. Arms of the bases should be kept close to the body. Thrust should be carried from the legs, through the shoulders, and up through the arms. Make sure that at the top of the stunt, the bases' arms are completely locked out and the bases are looking up at the flyer.

- When cradling, the bases use their legs, bending at the knees, and pop through the shoulders, flicking with their hands and fingers, to propel the flyer upward.

- As the bases are cradling, their arms stay extended to catch the flyer. When the flyer lands, the bases' arms immediately tighten to resist the downward movement of the flyer.

- When catching a cradle, base needs to absorb in her legs, not her back.

- A good beginning drill for the bases is simulating the stunt without the flyer. Often, the back spotter can be the "pretend flyer" by using her hands in place of the flyer and pressing downward.

Flyer (top person, climber, mounter, partner)

- Flyer should know how to fall.

- Flyer should never permit her feet to go more than shoulder-width apart.

- A good beginning drill for a flyer is step/lock.

- Loading into a stunt, the flyer must be aware of the initial weight distribution. Flyer must know when, where, and how to place her hands, feet, and other body parts on the base and she must be able to maintain balance.

- Flyer should hold her weight in her arms as she loads into a stunt. She should not bend her arms and let her bottom drop as she places her feet in the bases' hands. As bases dip, she must straighten and lock her body as the bases elevate her into the stunt. It is much easier for the bases to control a tight flyer than a loose, out-of-control body.

- As progression occurs, flyer needs to understand and master body alignment. Flyers should always keep their shoulders and hips square as though their body is in a cylinder or column. This concept prevents the body from falling out of alignment.

- Flyer must trust her bases. Her primary job is to maintain a tight, controlled, squared body.

Back Spotter (third base, rear spotter, third man, bracer)

- Back spotter is the most important person of the stunt. She is the one that controls the start and finish of the stunt. Most often, this cheerleader is the tallest person in the stunt group.

- Back spotter must watch the flyer's hips since they are the center of gravity for a flyer.

- Back spotter needs to be aggressive and have quick reflexes.

- Back spotter protects the flyer's head, neck, and shoulders while cradling.

Co-ed Stunting

This type of stunting is usually done with one girl as the flyer and one boy as the base. On the fully extended stunts, a separate spotter is needed. See examples under "Types of Stunts" later in this chapter.

Dismounts

Step-off

- Bases have hand-to-hand contact with the flyer and assist on the dismount.

- Flyer must keep body aligned and tight.

- Bases and back spotter must help to absorb the flyer's weight on the dismount by gripping her hands at the top of the stunt and catching her under the armpits with the inside hand (fingertips forward), as she dismounts to the ground.

Shove Wrap (pencil drop, bear hug, stomach wrap)

- The back spotter and two primary bases bend their knees and push the flyer's feet together.

- The flyer stays locked as her feet come together and drops straight down.

- The flyer should keep her arms clasped overhead for this dismount.

- The bases and back spotter bear hug the flyer on the way down, absorbing her weight.

Cradles

Most cradles are done with three people: two bases and a back spotter. Use counts so that everyone moves at the same time. The back spotter calls: "Cradle, 1, 2, down, up."

- The flyer can do arm movements in a number of different ways. In one common movement, the arms start in a high V position and, on the pop, reach up to a touchdown. In another common method, the arms start in a high V position and, on the pop, slap down to the flyer's side.

- In the air, the body of the flyer should stay straight or in a slight arch. Toes should be pointed.

- Upon landing in the cradle, the flyer's arm should hit a T or half-T. This movement will allow the third base to scoop and hold the flyer up higher.

- The bases should dip together on the "down" word and pop upward on "up."

- As bases catch, they should stop the flyer at chest height and bend the knees to cushion the cradle.

- Bases must not lean forward as they catch.

- Bases should not let the flyer's bottom go lower than the bases' waists.

- The back spotter holds the ankles or calves of the flyer and throws upward. As the back spotter throws, she should reach up with hands in blades until the flyer comes down. She then scoops under the armpits of the flyer, pulling the flyer into her chest. She should be careful not to hit the flyer in the face with her hands as she catches.

- Bases should watch the flyer at all times in case she starts to fall or lean in one direction.

- While stunting, a fourth base can be used (front spotter) if desired. She can hold the front wrist of the bases for stability. She can also help even out a bad pop as the bases dip and throw. Front spotter catches the legs of the flyer at the ankles during the cradle.

Load-Ins and Grips

When building a stunt, you must consider two crucial elements: how to get into the stunt and how the bases should place their hands to assist the flyer in the load-in. No absolute "right" way exists. Flyers can climb into the stunts in many ways. Bases can perform stunts using different hand grips. Experiment with the following methods for different stunts. Use the ones that work best for your team.

- *Load-In Grip (Figure 8-4)*—Bases bend their knees. Hands are cupped, palms facing upward.

Figure 8-5

Figure 8-4

Figure 8-6

- *Load-In Pop Grip (Figure 8-5)*—Secondary base cups the flyer's foot. Primary base places her right hand in between the secondary base's hands under the same foot. The flyer puts her left foot on the forearm of the primary base as she loads in.

- *Natural Grip (Figure 8-6)*—Used for prep, elevator, or full extension. Bases hold the foot of the flyer. They need to keep their wrists as close together as possible in order to provide a platform for the flyer to stand on.

- *Burrito or Sandwich Load-In Grip (Figure 8-7)*—One base places her hand under the flyer's foot and the other hand "sandwiches" the top of the foot.

- *Liberty Extended Grip (Figure 8-8)*—The "burrito grip" extended.

Figure 8-7

Figure 8-9

Figure 8-8

Figure 8-10

- *Vault Over Grip (Figure 8-9)*—Base faces forward and reaches overhead and grabs the flyer's hands. The flyer is standing behind the base.

- *Crisscross Grip (Figure 8-10)*—Bases cross their right hands over their left.

- *Handshake Grip (Figure 8-11)*—Base and flyer face each other. They "shake hands" with their right hands and extend their left arms up. They grab each other's left hand as if they are looking at their watches.

Figure 8-11

- *Four-Fingers-Forward Grip (Figure 8-12)*—With their fingertips forward, the bases grab under the armpits of the flyer.

Figure 8-12

- *Walk-in Grip (Figure 8-13)*—Flyer faces the base. She steps one foot into the hands of one base.

Figure 8-13

- *Thigh Stand Grip (Figure 8-14)*—Flyer steps a foot on the bases' thighs. Bases grab under the toe with their right hands and wrap their left arms around the flyer's knees.

Figure 8-14

- *Shoulder Stand Grip (Figure 8-15)*—Base reaches high on the flyer's calves and pulls down.

Figure 8-15

- *Basket Toss Grip (Figure 8-16)*—Bases grab their left wrists with their right hands. The bases lace the two hands together.

Figure 8-16

Types of Stunts

Below the Waist (Beginning)

Below-the-waist stunts are the most basic type of stunt. They are low-risk stunts that help the cheerleaders learn the importance of body alignment, trust, step-lock technique, spotting, and safety. All cheerleaders need to demonstrate their proficiency in the following below-the-waist stunts before moving on to the more difficult, advanced stunts. Document each successful completion of a stunt.

- *Double-Based Thigh Stand (Figure 8-17)*—Flyer steps onto one base's thigh and locks her knee, then places the other foot onto the second base's thigh. Bases grab under the flyer's toe and wrap their other arm above her knee.

- *Single-Based Thigh Stand (Figure 8-18)*—The flyer steps onto the base's thigh. The base wraps her arm above the flyer's knee and grabs under the flyer's foot with the other hand.

Figure 8-17

Figure 8-18

Shoulder Level (Intermediate)

- *Elevator (prep, extension prep) (Figure 8-19)*—Bases face inward with hands at knee level and backs straight. They bend their knees as the flyer steps into their hands and rides up to shoulder level.

- *Shoulder Stand (Figure 8-20)*—Flyer stands with one foot on either side of the base's head.

Figure 8-19

Figure 8-21

Figure 8-20

Figure 8-22

- *Shoulder Sit (Figure 8-21)*—Flyer straddles base's head and sits on her shoulders with legs wrapped under the base's armpits.

- *Chair (Figure 8-22)*—Flyer sits on the extended right hand of the base.

- *Toss Hands (Figure 8-23)*—Flyer is tossed from the ground to the hands of the base at shoulder level.

- *Torch (Figure 8-24)*—Flyer's hips and legs face the side while her upper torso faces forward. One foot is bent to the knee.

Figure 8-23 Figure 8-24

Fully Extended and Airborne (Advanced and Elite)

Only knowledgeable, well-trained squads that understand all the safety considerations and rules of elite-level building should perform fully extended and airborne stunts.

- *Overhead Straddle (Figure 8-25)*—Bases extend the flyer overhead with their hands on the flyer's ankle and thigh. Back base has her hands under the seat of the flyer. The flyer is in a seated V-sit position. This stunt needs another person (spotter) behind it.

Figure 8-25

- *Extended Flatback/Deadman's Lift (Figure 8-26)*—Flyer lies flat on her back as the bases extend her overhead.

Figure 8-26

- *Double-Base Full Extension (Figure 8-27)*—Same as "elevator" except bases fully extend flyer overhead.

Figure 8-27

- *Single-Base Full Extension (Figure 8-28)*—The flyer has her feet in the hands of one person (base).

Figure 8-28

Figure 8-29

Figure 8-30

- *Liberty (Figure 8-29)*—Fully extended stunt where the flyer is on one leg in the hands of the base(s) and her opposite leg is bent beside the supporting leg.

- *High Torch (Figure 8-30)*—Same as a liberty except flyer's hips and legs face the side while her upper torso faces forward.

- *Heel Stretch (Figure 8-31)*—An extended one-legged stunt where the flyer extends one leg diagonally up and grabs the heel.

- *Scorpion (Figure 8-32)*—An extended one-legged stunt where the flyer grabs one leg behind her head.

- *Scale (Figure 8-33)*—An extended one-legged stunt where the flyer extends a leg straight behind her and grabs that leg with her hand.

Figure 8-31

Figure 8-32

Figure 8-33

- *Arabesque (Figure 8-34)*—An extended one-legged stunt where the flyer extends the leg diagonally behind her. Note that the flyer should keep her torso up.

- *Awesome/Cupie (Figure 8-35)*—An extended stunt where the flyer's feet are together in the hands of her base(s).

- *Basket Toss (Figure 8-36)*—The flyer is tossed into the air and she performs a movement such as a toe touch, tuck-out, X-out, kick-out, or twist.

- *Cradle (Figure 8-37)*—See explanation under "Parts of a Stunt" earlier in this chapter.

- *Twist Cradle/Full-down (Figure 8-38)*—As the flyer is tossed into the air, she initiates one or two rotations. This move cannot be used in high school, where no overhead rotations are allowed.

- *Log or Barrel Roll (Figure 8-39)*—A flyer cradled in a horizontal position is tossed as she rotates parallel to the performing surface and is caught again by the original bases.

Figure 8-34

Figure 8-35

Figure 8-36

Figure 8-37

Figure 8-38

Figure 8-39

Pyramids

Joining several stunts together is a pyramid. As in stunts, pyramids can be simple or advanced depending on the ability of the squad. Once the team has mastered the basics, building pyramids is both fun and exciting.

To build a pyramid, select stunts to combine together. Be sure that your team has mastered these stunts individually before connecting them together. Also decide how the team will dismount from the stunts before constructing a pyramid. Because the mounts are built close together, choosing how to get out of the pyramid is key to safety. Walk through the building process with counts, only pretending to do the stunts. This exercise ensures that everyone thinks through the stages and understands each step. Once each step is mastered, then build the pyramid.

Transitional Stunts

Transitional stunts involve moving from one stunt to another. This type of stunting is used mostly in competition routines. Transitional stunts create a visual flow to your routine that adds energy and excitement. Some examples of transitional stunts include the following:

- *Show and Go/Instamatics*—This stunt "hits" at the top for an instant and then moves onto another stunt.

- *Retakes/Sponges (Figure 8-40)*—This stunt is performed at the "bottom" of the stunt where the flyer comes out of one stunt and shifts to another one, usually without her feet touching the ground.

Figure 8-40

- *Twist-in (Figure 8-41)*—Flyer faces the back spot. As she loads into the stunt, she crosses her legs and twists 180 degrees to the front. Both bases have their right hand over the left hand as flyer loads in and they rotate hands to standard prep/elevator grip as the flyer is turning.

- *Vault Over (Figure 8-42)*—Flyer is in an elevator/prep stunt. A person standing on the floor and facing towards the front grabs the hands of the flyer. The flyer jumps over the head of the front base as the primary two bases toss her feet. Then the two primary bases move in front of the front base as the flyer vaults over her. They catch the flyer's feet in a reload position.

- *Tictocs*—A one-legged stunt in which the flyer switches legs while being braced by a shoulder-level stunt.

Getting Technical Help

To learn stunts, you need hands-on help. Stunting is very visual. Attend camps and clinics with your cheerleaders. These classes are the best ways to learn proper technique and safety. Hire a professional instructor from a major cheerleading company to teach a private clinic for your cheerleaders. Check with your local college to see if one of the college cheerleaders can help with stunting. Ask a veteran coach to coach your team for a day. Another good resource are training videos such as *Fundamentals of Basic Stunting, Mastering Advanced Stunting*, and *Creating Excitement with Transitional Stunting*, all of which are available from Coaches Choice (www.coacheschoice.com).

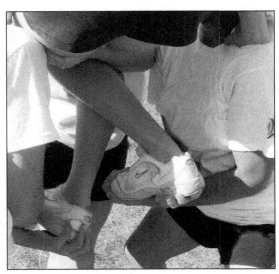

Figure 8-41

Figure 8-42

9

School Spirit

"No one keeps enthusiasm automatically. Enthusiasm must be nourished with new actions, new aspirations, new efforts, new visions."

—Papyrus

School spirit is a mixture of motivating the crowd at games, creating pride and unity in your school, supporting and motivating teams and athletes, and getting the community involved. This chapter will discuss each of these elements and detail how to accomplish them.

Motivating the Crowd

You want the crowd on their feet cheering for the team. How do you do that?

- Ask students, teachers, a leadership class, athletes, team parents, and the booster club what they need to make them cheer for the team. Write a spirit survey for the school newspaper asking students about their favorite spirit activity and request suggestions for upcoming games. Knowing that the cheerleaders care about them sometimes is enough to motivate them to cheer with the cheerleaders.

- On opening kickoff, have the crowd yell, starting low and getting louder as the kicker kicks the ball. Or have the cheerleaders in fully extended stunts with their arms overhead and waving side to side. Have the crowd imitate the same arm movements.

- Keep the cheers and chants simple. Story cheers are too hard to follow. The crowd needs short, catchy chants that they can easily learn and repeat.

- Use signs. A favorite is a big sign that says "Make Some Noise." When the cheerleaders hold it up, the crowd goes crazy. Use a sign that says "I Can't Hear You!" to encourage the audience to yell even louder. Other simple sign ideas are "Cheer With Us," "Get On Your Feet," "Louder," and, of course, the standard "Go," "Fight," "Win." Another great idea is a sign that rolls down as a cheerleader goes up in a fully extended stunt (Figures 9-1a and 9-1b).

- Get the crowd to move, which is often easier than having them yell words. Have signs that say, "Clap," "Stomp," and "Noise." Another idea is to have the cheerleaders do a hand jive for the crowd to imitate while the band plays.

- Use crowd participation chants.

- Use props, such as the following:

  Paint a sign with a big capital "D" on it and hold up a piece of fence with it. Yell "Defense" at the same time.

  Throw a huge beach ball painted in school colors into the crowd and have them toss it around to get them excited. Toss the beach ball into the crowd every time the team scores a touchdown. Take it away at kickoff.

Figure 9-1a

Figure 9-1b

Make a huge flag with school initials on it. As the team enters the field, the mascot or head cheerleader holds the flag and runs ahead of them onto the field. Announce for all the fans to stand on their feet and clap for the team.

Figure 9-2

Make large stretch pillowcases with your school's letters painted on the outside. Make them big enough for a cheerleader to fit inside (Figure 9-2).

- Create traditions at games. For example:

    Use the same cheer for free throws.

    Feature your fight song at each game.

    Use the crowd's favorite chant at timeouts.

    Do push-ups or jumps for each point scored at a football game.

    Make a reusable run-through banner for the team to bust through at halftime (Figure 9-3).

Figure 9-3

- Spotlight different groups to make them feel part of the game. Advertise to that featured group in advance so they will come to the game. Some groups to honor include parents, teachers, the community, and youth sport leagues.

- Work on your cheerleaders' crowdleading skills. Make sure they use big, bold moves. Have them make eye contact with the crowd. If at first a new idea does not work, don't give up. Remember that cheerleaders need to always project a fun, enthusiastic appearance.

Creating Pride in Your School

One of the fundamental jobs of cheerleaders is to build excitement for the upcoming games. If cheerleaders can get the students involved in this enthusiasm, the students will develop a sense of pride for their school and its sport teams. Sell spirit items like mini-megaphones, foam #1 hands, mini pompons, spirit rags in school colors, and glow sticks and necklaces with a tag that says, "Let your spirit shine!" Often, you can have community businesses sponsor the cost of these items and then you can give them away for free.

Posters and Signs

Displaying fun signs throughout the school is a great way to motivate the students. See Figure 9-4 for instructions on making superior signs. Decorate the halls, school, and stadium with posters for upcoming games. Poster ideas include the following:

- *Spirit Board*—A place where all the upcoming activities are posted. It could be a large calendar with dates, times, and place of the events or a poster with a list of activities. Use a digital camera to take pictures of the teams and post them on the board.

- *Spirit Ladder*—Paint a ladder (or a big ladder-size poster) in school colors and decorate it with the school's mascot on top. On each rung, put the name of the opponents in order, starting with the first opponent on the bottom rung.

- *Spread the News*—Decorate the wall with newspapers and write on top of the newspaper: "Spread the news, the Wildcats are gonna beat the _____."

- *Yard Signs*—Make a bunch of yard signs about the upcoming game. Do a theme or series of messages.

- *Stomp Out the_____*—This poster could be in the shape of a paw. Put this big poster on the floor for everyone entering the school to walk on.

- *Upcoming Game*—Make a sign in the shape of a football, soccer ball, or volleyball. List the date, time, and location of each upcoming game as it approaches.

Tips for Making Superior Signs

- Make them big and bold.

- Keep them simple with lettering that is clear and easy to read.

- Make signs very visual to grab people's attention. Use color and interesting graphics.

- Make a border at least one inch wide on all sides of the poster. For best results, draw the border slightly wider at the bottom of the poster.

- Use consistent lettering. Select a style that is easy to read and not too fancy. Limit the lettering styles to no more than three per poster. Capital letters outlined in contrasting colors are best on a sign. Slant letters up for effect. Lettering height should be the same within a word. When working on white paper, colors of letters should be dark and outlined in brighter colors (like yellow). Use colors that contrast to accentuate the words. Don't crowd the letters or words.

- Plan the layout of your poster before starting. Keep the layout simple. Organize graphics, lines, words, and lettering so that they are balanced.

- Use materials that are durable and sturdy. Consider laminating posters to use multiple times.

- Include all essential information. Be specific and not too wordy. The reader should be able to take in all the information in a matter of seconds.

- Pay attention to details. Check spelling and grammar. Keep the poster neat.

- Vary the shapes and types of the posters: boxes, flags, long, short, folding, ones that open like a book, etc.

Figure 9-4

- *Player Recognition*—Make a giant paper football field out of poster paper and put mini-helmets on it with the name and number of each player. Display on the wall. For other sports, use the following: soccer field with little balls, pool with swimsuits, net with volleyballs, net with tennis balls, megaphone with mini-poms, basketball court with mini-basketballs.

- *Giant Megaphone*—Make a giant megaphone and display it in the hallway. List the spirit winners of the week on it.

- *Cheer of the Week*—Have a special location in the school where you hang a poster or banner with the words to the cheer of the week for all the students to read and learn before the game.

- *Follow the Footprints*—Cut paws or footprints from butcher paper to "pave" the way to the big pep rally or game!

- *Let's Get Fired Up!*—Write these words on a poster with flames of fire around them.

- *Wildcats Are Unstoppable*—Draw these words on a big stop sign.

- *Spirit Fence*—Paint Styrofoam cups with your school colors. Pull the cups through the holes in a chain-link fence at the stadium and spell out spirit slogans and mascot name. Another way to decorate a fence is to tie colored ribbon on it to either spell out words or form a picture.

Get the Word Out

Students won't go to the games unless they know the sport schedule. In addition to posters, publicize events in other ways, such as the following: distribute pocket sports calendars, print the list of games in the student handbook, use sandwich boards, make P.A. announcements, and advertise the sport schedule in the school newspaper.

Contests

Best Fan in the Stands—The cheerleaders pick an adult and a student who display the most spirit during the game. Announce the winner between the third and fourth quarters. Give each person a t-shirt that says "Best Fan in the Stands."

Backward Chant—Read a chant backwards over the intercom and have students guess the chant. Give a prize to the first person that turns in the right answer.

Guess the Poms—Stuff a bunch of pompons in a large, clear container. Then set the container in an open area where students can guess how many poms are inside the container. The winner receives a pair of poms and free admission to the big game!

Spirit Links—Sell strips of construction paper (different colors for each class) to students for 25 cents each. Make a chain for each class by stapling the strips together and, at a pep assembly, hide all the class chains in a box. Playing suspenseful music, slowly pull out each class chain. The class with the longest chain receives the amount of money collected for the chains. Then, have the football team play tug-of-war with the chains and give a prize to the person whose name appears on the spot where the chain breaks.

Spirit Couch—Every time a student demonstrates school spirit, a cheerleader writes their name on a spirit ticket. At the end of the week, draw one name from the spirit tickets. That person gets to sit on the spirit couch at the game with a friend of their choice and is served pizza at halftime.

Bet on a Victory—At a pep rally, play a dice game with representatives from each class, the sport team, and the teachers. Tape off a six by six grid on the floor.

Name each lane: freshmen, sophomores, juniors, seniors, teachers, and football players, and assign a number to each lane. The goal is to be the first person to advance through the grid, moving ahead one box at a time. Roll a large pair of dice. The number rolled indicates which lane can move. Before the pep rally, make a spirit box for each group and put the boxes in the front office or the student leadership class. Then hide paper money with the school mascot on it around the school. When a person finds it, he can bet on who will win the dice game at the upcoming pep rally by writing his name on the money and putting it in one of the spirit boxes. After the game, pull a name from the winning group's box and give that person a prize.

Traditions

- All the students wear school colors on game days.

- The students paint their faces for the big game.

- Host a tailgate party before the game starts.

- Find a team song and play it at all their games.

- Each class creates a class chant or song.

- Organize a snake dance through town before the homecoming game.

- Decorate the town with balloons in school colors.

- Ask local businesses to display the upcoming game on their marquee.

- Decorate players' yards with signs and banners.

- Place a teacher appreciation cake in the teachers' lounge once a quarter.

- Play the school fight song every morning before announcements.

- Use run-through signs at halftime.

- Have a "spirit jug." Every time the jug is uncorked, have the crowd yell!

Pep Rallies

Have short assemblies to fire up the students for the upcoming game. Pep rallies instill pride, boost spirit, give recognition, build unity, showcase talent, and teach appropriate school behavior and sportsmanship. Keep the whole event to 30 minutes or less. You want the crowd to leave wanting more! (Refer to Figures 9-5 and 9-6.)

Incorporate school clubs in your pep rallies. Club members could lead the class competition or perform a mini-skit. Always have the band playing while the students are entering and leaving the pep rally. Music sets the mood! Put up a big backdrop for the cheerleaders, emcee, and sports teams to stand in front of during the assembly. Set standards and teach the students that sportsmanship starts with their school. For a good pep rally, remember the three Ps: planning, practice, and performance.

Aside from planning, the crucial element to a good pep assembly is imagination. Design a theme for your rally to generate excitement (theme ideas are provided later in this chapter under "Spirit Week"). You want to grab their attention. You need a dynamic emcee that can inspire the entire student body. A few ways guaranteed to liven up the crowd are the following:

Pep Rally Checklist

Assembly Date: _____

Person in Charge: _____

☐ Format

☐ Agenda (Send to all participants and administrators)

☐ Gym, room, or field set-up (bleachers, decorations)

☐ Sound system request

☐ Notification of all participants

☐ List of supplies and equipment

☐ Rehearsal time and date

☐ Music selection

☐ Script for emcee and skits

☐ Clean-up

☐ Thank you notes

Notes:

Figure 9-5

<table>
<tr><td colspan="2" align="center">**Pep Rally Schedule**</td></tr>
<tr><td>1:30 pm</td><td>Students enter. Band is playing and cheerleaders are dancing on the sidelines.</td></tr>
<tr><td>1:40 pm</td><td>Emcee welcomes everyone. (This person needs to be full of enthusiasm and energy.) She leads the crowd in the Pledge of Allegiance.</td></tr>
<tr><td>1:45 pm</td><td>Cheerleaders lead the crowd in a cheer or chant.</td></tr>
<tr><td>1:50 pm</td><td>As the emcee introduces the sport team, the band plays a theme song like "Bad to the Bone" or "Superman." The coach gives a brief pep talk.</td></tr>
<tr><td>2:00 pm</td><td>Fun skit or class competition.</td></tr>
<tr><td>2:10 pm</td><td>Everyone sings the school fight song. Emcee dismisses the crowd.</td></tr>
</table>

Figure 9-6

- *Scavenger Hunt*—Pick a team of four from each class and give them a list of items to find in the audience. As they are searching, announce on the microphone what these items are.

- *Audience Art*—Select a team of four people from each class. Give them supplies to decorate a class spirit poster. Set a time limit and then let the audience decide which poster is the best.

- *TP a Teacher*—Ask four teachers to volunteer to be wrapped in toilet paper. Choose two students from each class and see who can wrap the teacher totally in toilet paper first. The students have to use the entire roll.

- *Mix Up Shoes*—Have five students from each class remove their shoes and place them in a pile in the center of the gym. Place each person on different sides of the gym. In two minutes, the students have to find their shoes, lace them up, and return to their beginning spot.

- *Rap Contest*—Have one student from each class demonstrate a rap-type cheer. Award prizes to the winner.

- *Sumo Wrestling*—Rent two padded sumo wrestling costumes. Have the freshmen compete against the sophomores and juniors compete against the seniors. The winners compete against each other.

Spirit Week

Usually, Spirit Week is the week of Homecoming. Each day, the students dress up in the theme of the day. Dress up a mannequin in the theme and display her in the cafeteria or front hallway. You can have a separate theme each day of the week or one theme for the entire week with sub-themes for each day. Give prizes or spirit points to the class that has the most students participating.

Week Themes

- Tis the Season—Each day of the week centers around a different holiday

- Sports Center—Every day focuses on one sport

- Blast from the Past—Each day's theme is a different decade

- Pride in America—Each day features a branch of the military

- Around the World in Five Days—Each day focuses on a different country

Day Themes

- Backwards Day
- Career Day
- International Day
- Cartoon Day
- Stripe Day
- Character Day
- Twin Day
- Wacky Hair Day
- Color Day
- College Color Day
- Western Day
- Crazy Shoe Day
- Camouflage Day
- Mismatch Day

- Dress-up Day
- Jungle Day
- Formal Day
- Costume Day
- Funky Hair Day
- Hat Day
- Hawaiian Day
- Inside-out Day
- Movie Day
- Farm Day
- Pajama Day
- Plaid Day
- Wig Day
- TV Star Day

Motivating the Athletes

- Decorate bulletin boards for each sport. Post photos, win-loss records, newspaper articles, special awards, and motivational sayings.

- Recognize an "Athlete of the Week."

- Schedule a "Meet the Team" night.

- Structure pep rallies to include a section featuring the athletes.

- Give spirit treats as a special way to support and acknowledge athletes. Some ideas include the following:

  "Breakfast of Champions"—Decorate mini Wheaties cereal boxes with photos of each player.

  Spirit Candy Bars—Create a school logo and wrap it around candy bars.

  Luggage Tags—Make a personalized spirit design on white card stock, laminate, punch a hole in one end, and attach a luggage loop.

  Can-Dos—Decorate cans, fill with candy, and add notes that say, "You CAN do it!" or "Success comes in CANS not cannots."

  Fill toilet paper rolls with goodies and wrap them in paper with a pipe cleaner tied at each end. Write, "Our team is dynamite!" on the paper.

  Distribute $100,000 candy bars that say, "You're worth a grand."

Hand out PowerBars with a note that says, "You've got the power to win."

Fill plastic Easter eggs with candy and add a note that says "Thanks for your 'eggs'tra effort at last night's game!"

Blow Pops—"Blow away the competition!"

Fireball Candies—"Wildcats are fired up!"

Spirit Sticks—Licorice in school colors.

Now and Later Candy— "Beat 'em now and celebrate later."

Red Hots Candy—"Wildcats are red hot!"

Spirit Towels—Create a special game towel for each athlete. Personalize with fabric paint.

Pillowcases—Decorate pillowcases with fabric paint for each player and coach to use on overnight trips (e.g. playoffs or championship games).

A Bag of Potato Chips—"You're all that and a bag of chips."

Play Money—"Bet the Wildcats will win tonight!"

Balloons—"The sky's the limit for the mighty Wildcats."

Starburst Candy—"Wildcats are superstars tonight! Good luck!"

Picnic Goody Basket—Collect food for a team that has to travel a distance to a game.

Locker Poster—Put decorated posters on the lockers of the players wishing them good luck at the upcoming game. Examples include:

o Clock decoration—"It's time for a victory."

o A sign in the shape of a paper bag—"Sack the Badgers."

o Hat decoration—"Hats off to the best team in the district!"

- Lightning bolt—"Charge up for a victory."

- "Victory is our battle cry."

- A picture of a football field covered with rain—"Wildcats will reign over the field!"

- Drawing of the opposing mascot in a box—"Wrap'em up."

Get the Community Involved

- Send articles about your teams to the local newspaper and PTA newsletters.

- Have businesses display the date of the big game on their store marquee.

- Host tailgate parties for the community before the game.

- Parade through town on the way to the game.

- Make a sport poster calendar and have businesses display them in their store window.

- Throw out spirit items with business advertising on them at games.

- Feature a business of the week at each game.

- Invite the local media to a pep rally.

- Decorate the town with balloons in school colors during Homecoming week.

- Include alumni in your Homecoming assembly.

- Include alumni cheerleaders at the Homecoming game.

- Make spirit buttons for parents with their player's photo on it.

- Organize a parent pep club.

- Have a food drive at the game.

- Contact the local merchants and plan a window-painting contest.

Lastly, to get the community involved in the schools, cheerleaders need to be involved in the community. Help out when asked. Cheerleaders can lend a helping hand in many places, such as senior centers, youth centers, parades, and local community-sponsored charity affairs and fundraisers. Cheerleaders should always be a part of events like Red Ribbon Week in October and National Night Out in August. Offer your squad's services to grand openings of new businesses and volunteer to perform for local hospitals or at schools for mentally disabled children. Teach at elementary after-school enrichment programs. Encourage your cheerleaders to assist and help wherever they can.

10

Game Day Considerations

*"When you're prepared, you're more confident
When you have a strategy, you're more comfortable."*

—Fred Couples

It's game day. Are your cheerleaders ready? Are you, as the coach, ready? Have you taken care of all the loose ends? As always, when you are dealing with students and parents, planning is essential.

Game Guidelines

Guidelines should include proper procedures for cheerleaders at games. It is best that all cheerleaders have a copy of these game rules in their cheerleading notebook and that the coach has a signed copy from every athlete in her files. See Figure 10-1 for a sample copy of game guidelines.

Teach cheerleaders what they need to do at a game. Their first game can be both scary and exciting. The more you prepare them, the better they can handle most situations. Drill your cheerleaders over and over at practice until they know the cheers and chants completely. They need to feel confident with their material so that they can concentrate on leading the crowd. Teach them to jump and rally if their mind goes blank when a chant is called, instead of standing there looking like a scared rabbit. Keep a laminated copy of the chant list at the games for reference. Determine chant lines or game formations at practice. The standard sideline chant procedure is to have a captain start the words, and have the rest of the squad join in for the last half of the chant while pumping the crowd. Then the second time through, everyone does the motions. Continue chanting until

Game Expectations

- Arrive at facility 45 minutes prior to game time. You have a five-minute grace period. If you arrive after that time, you will sit out the first half beside your coach and cheer from the stands.
- Warm up for the first 15 minutes.
- Review necessary material for 15 minutes.
- Be ready to cheer 15 minutes before the start of the game.
- Travel in school transportation when required.
- Be dressed and ready upon arrival.
- Wear NO jewelry and have hair pulled up (out of the face and off the shoulders).
- Have complete uniform, neat and clean, at all games. If you do not have the proper uniform, you will be unable to cheer. You will sit out the game beside your coach and cheer from the stands.
- Have all uniform pieces with you at all games.
- Remain in cheering area during the game.
- Follow the game plan.
- Execute chants and routines correctly.
- Control and lead the crowd through organized cheers and chants. Display correct and acceptable leadership skills.
- Do not socialize with players or crowd members during the game.
- Follow the captains. Do not tell them what chants you want or do not want to do.
- Do not act silly. Remember that you are an athlete.
- Follow the coach's directive.
- Do not chew gum.
- Perform only the stunts that have been perfected and only if the coach is present. All stunts need to have the proper amount of spotters.
- Do not interfere with the players or officials.
- Promote sportsmanship.

Figure 10-1

the captain yells "last time." The cheerleaders should face the game when not cheering to the fans so they know what is happening. Have a signal that tells the cheerleaders when to turn back to face the audience.

It is very important for the cheerleaders to know when to cheer during a game, for example:

- Always cheer *for* your team and never against the other team.

- Cheer as the team enters the field or the court.

- Cheer during the introduction of players.

- Cheer when a substitution is made for your team.

- Cheer when your team makes a great play.

- Cheer as an encouragement for your team to make a score or defend their goal.

- Cheer as a means to discourage negative remarks or booing from the fans.

It is equally important for the cheerleaders to know when not to cheer, for example:

- Never cheer when a player is injured. Most squads bend down on one knee during the injury and stand up and applaud courteously when the player leaves the field.

- Never cheer when the ball is being served in volleyball.

- Never use artificial noisemakers or noise enhancers at indoor sports. Check with your athletic director to know if cheerleaders are permitted to use megaphones. If they are, only direct them to the fans.

- Never cheer when a basketball player is attempting a free throw.

- Never cheer when an opposing player makes a mistake.

- Never cheer when an unsportsmanlike act has occurred.

- Do not go onto the basketball court and cheer during 30-second timeouts. It is, however, permissible to cheer from the sidelines.

- Do not set up your cheer lines under the basketball backboard during the game.

- Never interfere with the officials. Stay out of their way.

- Do not stunt when the ball is in play during basketball and volleyball games.

Review and answer the following questions for cheerleaders before every game:

- What time should the team arrive?

- Where should they meet?

- What should they wear?

- Where will they warm up?

- Where will they cheer?

- Where are the spirit supplies and who will bring them to the game?

- When should they cheer and when should they not cheer?

- Who will call the chants?

- Who will coordinate with the band?

- What will the team perform at halftime or quarters?

- Who will coordinate with the announcer?

- Who will run the music if needed?

- When will the cheerleaders line up by the goalpost for the run-through at halftime?

- Where will the trainer, administrator, and security officer be during the game?

Game Plan

Assign a cheerleader to complete a game plan or agenda for each game. Review it at the last practice before the game. Of course, cheerleaders will need to be flexible and adapt their plans to the situation and weather. Refer to Figure 10-2.

Game Plan

1. _____ brings treats for opposing team's cheerleaders

2. _____ brings signs for _____ game

    Signs include: _____

                                         _____

                                         _____

                                         _____

3. Stunts to use: _____

_____

_____

_____

_____

_____

_____

4. _____ brings spirit items for _____ game

    Spirit items include: _____

                                           _____

                                           _____

                                           _____

5. _____ brings run-through to _____ game

6. _____ will handle the announcements and music for half-time

Routine for half-time is _____

_____

_____

7. _____ brings list of defense, offense, and general chants.

8. _____ will call the chants.

9. _____ will clean up at the end of the game.

Comments/Suggestions:

Figure 10-2

At all games, you, as the coach, should be in clear sight of the cheerleaders. They need to be able to look to you for direction and support. Be an active coach, not just one who sits in the audience socializing. Track what works and what needs improvement. Huddle with the cheerleaders to help with the game plan, add encouragement, or direct changes. These meetings are the equivalent of timeouts in other sports. Complete game day evaluations (Figure 10-3) for the squad to review at the next practice. Use the evaluations as a learning tool to help improve their crowdleading and cheer skills. At the end of every game, tell each cheerleader at least one positive remark about how she cheered.

Leading the Crowd

The primary focus of your cheerleaders is leading the crowd and promoting school spirit. The following components are needed to accomplish this big task:

Game Day Evaluation

Date _____ Game _____ Location _____

READINESS

Everyone has proper uniform.	Yes No
Everyone has hair up.	Yes No
No one is wearing jewelry.	Yes No

OVERALL GAME PERFORMANCE

Entrance	5 4 3 2 1	Tumbling	5 4 3 2 1
Spirit	5 4 3 2 1	Smiles	5 4 3 2 1
Use of signs	5 4 3 2 1	Voices	5 4 3 2 1
Jumps	5 4 3 2 1	Dancing	5 4 3 2 1
Interaction with fans	5 4 3 2 1	Sportsmanship	5 4 3 2 1

CHEERS/STUNTS

Crowd-oriented	5 4 3 2 1	Formation	5 4 3 2 1
Sharp motions	5 4 3 2 1	Knowledge of material	5 4 3 2 1
Climbing technique	5 4 3 2 1	Perfection of stunts	5 4 3 2 1
Timing	5 4 3 2 1		

CAPTAINS

Called chants in a timely manner.	5 4 3 2 1
Understood the game.	5 4 3 2 1
Maintained enthusiasm.	5 4 3 2 1
Incorporated stunts and tumbling.	5 4 3 2 1

COMMENTS

Need to improve:

Worked well:

Figure 10-3

- Cheerleaders must understand the dynamics of the sport. Teach the squad to read the scoreboard. At practice, review the rules of all sports.

- Signs are a great way to grab the crowd's attention. Often, at a football game, the cheerleaders are on a track that is a distance away from the crowd or they are separated from the crowd by a fence. Picture this situation: 15 seconds are left on the clock in the last quarter. Your team is up by three points. The opposing team is on the five-yard line and it is the fourth down. The cheerleaders want to rally the crowd behind the football team with a defense yell. Because the announcer is relaying facts and figures of the game, the cheerleaders might not be heard. If they hold up a big, bold sign that says "DEFENSE" as they start the defense chant, the audience is more likely to join in.

- When using signs, cheerleaders need to show the word before they want the crowd to say it. They should hold the sign in front of the body, with the word facing outward. When the time comes for the fans to yell, the cheerleaders extend the sign overhead and tilt it slightly forward. Cheerleaders often tilt it backwards, making it hard to see.

- If the crowd starts a supportive chant, encourage the cheerleaders to participate. Many times, cheerleaders think they have to initiate all chants. If the crowd is displaying school spirit, support it!

- Keep chants short and easy to follow. Often, cheerleaders only repeat a chant three times. In the crowd's mind, they hear it the first time, understand it the second time, and start yelling with the cheerleaders the third time. It can become frustrating to the crowd if they just started yelling and suddenly the cheerleaders stop. When calling chants, continue yelling the words until the audience loses interest in participating.

- Work with your band. Music is a powerful motivator.

- Get your cheerleaders as close to the crowd as possible. In some areas, cheerleaders stand on large wooden boxes in order to be seen better.

- Give out "spirit sticks" (licorice in school colors) to the students that yell the loudest.

- Throw spirit items like footballs, Frisbees, and spirit poms into the audience when the fans are cheering loudly.

- Use your mascot to motivate the crowd.

- Enlist the help of pep clubs and dance/drill teams.

- Use poms (see Figure 10-4). They are great attention-getters!

- Teach a new chant at a pep rally.

- Use the team's friends to teach chants in the stands.

- Lead with confidence. Cheerleaders are a powerful group; have them use their positions to rock the stands!

- Refer to "Motivating the Crowd" in Chapter 9 for more ideas.

- At a practice, brainstorm ideas with your cheerleaders for different ways to motivate the crowd. Use this activity to get the ideas flowing. Tell the cheerleaders to imagine walking into a

Figure 10-4

gym of a basketball game and hearing the most astonishing, high-spirited group of students. Now, divide the group of cheerleaders into three or four teams. Each squad records the "sights," "sounds," and "feelings" of the imagined game. Give the teams 15 minutes to write down their responses. Tell them to be specific and descriptive. Next, have each team share their ideas as one of the cheerleaders writes the responses on a large whiteboard. Discuss which items the cheerleaders can influence, what groups in the school can help the cheerleaders make other concepts happen, and whether any items on the list require permission and support from the administrators and teachers.

Sportsmanship

Sportsmanship and citizenship are words that are interchangeable. For schools, these words refer to proper conduct at any school events. The cheerleaders play an important part in helping students, teachers, and parents to display good sportsmanship. Sportsmanship is one of the strongest educational lessons and lifetime values taught by interscholastic athletics. Check with your school to see if they have a written sportsmanship policy. If so, be sure to look it over for information about the roles of the cheerleaders. If your school does not have a written policy, form a committee of students, teachers, administrators, and community members to write one. It should include the following:

- Sportsmanship and citizenship resolution

- Procedures for promoting the plan

- Sportsmanship rules for athletes, coaches, and spectators

- Good sportsmanship recognition program

- Procedures for handling poor sportsmanship

Obviously, cheerleaders play a key role in helping to uphold a sportsmanship policy and its applications. Some general rules for sportsmanship at school are the following:

- Do unto others as you would have them do to you.

- Be responsible for your actions.

- Have pride in your performance and your school.

- Be respectful of others.

- Accept the decisions of the officials.

- Applaud during the introductions of the players and coaches of both teams, as well as the officials.

- Remember it is a privilege to participate.

- Encourage others to do their best.

- Applaud at the end of the contest, no matter who wins.

- Cheer only in a positive manner.

- Never cheer against another team.

- Work in harmony with other cheerleaders.

- Think before you speak; never boo.

- Avoid facial expressions that show disagreements.

- Never use profanity or name-calling.

- Do not mock the other team, their fans, or their cheerleaders.

- Play fair and follow the rules.

- Remember that actions speak louder than words.

- Never blame the officials for losing a game.

Cheerleaders should make sportsmanship posters and place them around the halls, gym, and stadium. Write sportsmanship announcements for the games and PA system. Have a column in the school newspaper recognizing groups who demonstrate good sportsmanship. Give rewards (pens, coupons, movie passes) for positive actions.

In addition to encouraging sportsmanlike behavior, cheerleaders need to learn how to stop bad behavior at sporting events. When the crowd starts to boo or yell at a referee or display unsportsmanlike behavior, your cheerleaders should do one of the following:

- Start a popular chant to get the crowd yelling with them.

- Send a small group of cheerleaders into the crowd to start a crowd-involvement activity.

- Request that several administrators or teachers sit in the stands near the disruptive group.

- Charm the crowd into following in a cheer. Make eye contact and show them that their help is needed. Give them a prize for helping.

- Do not argue with hecklers. Ignore them. Be a positive role model.

Prepare your cheerleaders to handle unsportsmanlike situations by doing some role-playing games. At practice, talk about some situations that might occur. Discuss which ones the cheerleaders can manage and how. Decide which ones are best controlled by an administrator and which situations are best to just ignore.

Lastly, practice what you preach. Remind the cheerleaders that they are role models. Their actions speak louder then their words. Always meet and greet the opposing team's cheerleaders. Show them where to cheer, where the restrooms are, where to warm up, and where an administrator is standing in case they need help. Provide them with a small treat and drink as a thank-you for coming to your school. Sometimes, both spirit groups perform together at halftime. At the end of the game, be sure to stop by and thank them again for attending. The visiting cheerleaders should always leave your school feeling good about their time there.

Use of Mascot

Your mascot symbolizes school spirit and plays a key role in promoting and enhancing it. He can use large, exaggerated motions, silly antics, and fun skits to capture the crowd's attention. The mascot needs to develop a personality that the school will recognize and respond to. This person can be created with the way he walks, what he wears, and how he behaves. The mascot supports the cheerleaders, is friendly to both teams and their fans, promotes sportsmanship, and never fights with the other team's mascot. He must be animated, enthusiastic, and creative. He should never talk while in costume. Everything is a pantomime. He should never take any part of the costume off in public. The mascot should never stunt and can only perform forward rolls and cartwheels.

Include the mascot in your cheer practices in order to coordinate game day activities, performances, and special events. The mascot also needs to stay fit like the cheerleaders. Remember that the mascot is part of your team and you need to apply the same care and safety rules to him as you do to your cheerleaders.

The mascot should drink plenty of fluids before, during, and after the game or pep rally. The person inside the costume usually has very limited field of vision. Therefore, it is best to have another person with him at all times. Instruct the mascot to be especially careful not to scare children.

Some fun ways to use the mascot include the following:

- Have him lead the football players out of the locker room and onto the field.

- Have him get the crowd to do the wave.

- Have a "Photo with the Mascot" Night for a fundraiser for a local charity.

- He can roll out the red carpet for the players or cheerleaders.

- He can use a broom and "sweep the way" for their entrance.

- He can calm a rowdy crowd with silly antics.

- He can have a suitcase or trunk full of costumes and props (e.g., stick horse, big sunglasses, bowtie, silly hats, lasso, big handkerchief, flash cards, a mute horn) to use during timeouts.

- He can give out balloons or spirit items to children and fans.

- He can escort the principal or an important community member, like the mayor, to his seat.

- He can handle the "spirit jug." Every time he takes the cork off the top, the crowd yells. When he places it back on the jug, they are quiet.

Arrangements for Away Game

Transportation—At the beginning of the season, fill out all the appropriate forms for traveling: vehicle requests, cheerleader's permission slips to travel (Figure 10-5), and parent driver permission forms (Figure 10-6).

Emergency Plans—Remember to carry your emergency kit, plans, and forms with you to away games. Also. have the school's transportation phone number with you, in case you break down on the road. Keep a list of traveling cheerleaders in your vehicle with you and leave one at your school with an administrator.

Teach your cheerleaders what to do in case of emergency. If you go over what is expected of everyone in an emergency situation, it will make for a greater sense of preparedness. Take the time to talk about what each person's job would be in the event of an emergency on the road or at a visiting school. Plan ahead!

Destination—Do you know where you are going? Take the extra time to log on to the Internet to get precise directions to your destination. It can be very stressful driving around trying to find a high school in an unfamiliar town. You can't always look for the football field lights to find your way—you just might end up at an airport.

Make a list of questions to ask when you arrive at the visiting school. Often, time is short and if you have a written list of the normal things cheerleaders need to know, it will make cheering at a different school much easier for your athletes. Ask the following questions:

- Where do we warm up?

- Where do we cheer?

- Where are the restrooms?

Parent Driver Release Form

I agree to drive and supervise the following students

_____   _____

_____   _____

_____   _____

_____   _____

on a field trip to _____

on _____. I certify that I hold a current valid _____

driver's license. I understand the _____ School District is in no way responsible for any liability or property damage or for the repair of any damage done to my vehicle.

_____   _____

Signature   Date

Figure 10-5

Parent Permission for Student Travel

Name of Student:_____

Date(s) of Trip:_____   Supervisor:_____

Destination: Town:_____   Place:_____

Activity:_____

TRANSPORTATION
(check appropriate category)

_____ District Vehicle/Employee Driver   _____ District Vehicle/Non-employee Driver

_____ Private Vehicle/Student Driver   _____ Private Vehicle/Parent Driver

_____ Private Vehicle/District Employee Driver _____ Private Vehicle/Adult Volunteer Driver

_____ Private Carrier

   I give permission for the above-named student to participate in the above-mentioned activity. I understand that students are expected to remain with the group unless written permission is given by me to do otherwise.

HOLD HARMLESS

   In consideration of this student being allowed to participate in the above activity, I agree to hold the district harmless from any claim by or against it arising out of any negligent or wrongful action by the student.

   I give permission for the school to seek the services of a licensed medical person in the case of an accident or illness requiring medical aid for this student.

In the space below, please give any special instructions such as medication being taken, allergies to food or drugs, special diets, or any other medical problems we need to be aware of.

_____   _____
Parent/Legal Guardian Signature   Student

_____   _____
Relationship   Telephone (home and work)

_____   _____
Street Address   City, State, Zip Code

Please give the name and telephone number of a relative or friend who can be contacted in case of an emergency if you cannot be reached.

_____   _____
Name   Telephone

Figure 10-6

- Who performs at each quarter?

- Do we need to know any certain rules?

- Can we stunt?

- Where do we stand for the Pledge to the Flag?

- Where is the game manager if we need assistance?

- If we have more questions, whom do we ask?

- Do you have a trainer that we can use in case of emergency?

- Where is the closest place to get ice?

- What is the emergency number for medical assistance?

Weather—Check the forecast and prepare your cheerleaders for the elements. Weather can affect your routine. Do not allow your cheerleaders to stunt in the rain or extreme cold. Make sure they are dressed appropriately. Sometimes, their uniforms won't do. In cold or rainy climates, order warm-ups or rain jackets for them to wear when the weather gets bad.

Schedules—Distribute schedules to the cheerleaders and parents. Put everything in writing: when they are to arrive at the school, when they will leave for the away game, what time they are expected to be back. Carry a cell phone. Have your cheerleaders call while you are traveling home to let their parents know exactly when they are going to be ready to be picked up. When you get back to school, especially late at night, it is much nicer to have the parents waiting for you than for you to have to wait for the parents.

11

Competition

"Our goal is not to win. It is to play together and play hard. Then the winning takes care of itself."

—Mike Krzyzewski

The term *competition* refers to a group of cheerleaders performing a timed, choreographed routine that includes tumbling, cheering, stunting, jumping, and dancing in front of an audience and a panel of judges. Cheerleading competitions can be a positive means to motivating the team to achieve a higher degree of excellence in their skills, as well as a great lesson in teamwork.

Physical Preparation

In order to build a good competition routine, cheerleaders need to have perfected the required skills. Spend time developing these building blocks before teaching cheerleaders the competition routine. Start early in the year with the basics. Create an atmosphere of perfection before progression. Work jumps, arm motions, dance movements, tumbling, and stunts. Use game time and pep assemblies to perform skills that will be used later in the competition routine.

Mental Preparation

Attitude is the most important part of competing. Prepare your team by developing a "we can" attitude. Everyone needs to work together in order to be successful. Make sure everyone understands the time commitment needed to succeed. Set realistic personal and team goals and develop a plan to meet those goals.

Each member of a competition squad might have a different opinion of what success is. Ask your squad the following questions in order to understand the team's definition of success. Is success:

- Winning or placing?

- Placing at a particular number of competitions?

- Hitting a clean routine?

- Gaining experience?

- Having fun?

- Performing better at each event?

- A combination of ideas?

After answering these questions, your squad can better define success. Include short- and long-term goals in the team's definition of success. Working toward these goals helps them develop self-esteem through competition.

Teach your cheerleaders how competitions are structured. Walk them through the day of the event and tell them how it will run from start to finish. Prepare them to be adaptable because each venue is a little different. Show videos from competitions in your area or take them to watch one before they actually compete.

Give the squad a chance to perform the routine in front of an audience before they compete. They can perform at a football or basketball halftime, at a school assembly, or in front of the parents or community. Repetition helps the cheerleaders become more comfortable with the routine and that leads to more self-confidence.

To create a rewarding experience from competition, teach the team to compete against the scoresheet, not other teams. Scoring is very subjective, making it hard to predict the outcome of a competition. Cheerleaders cannot control the results, but they can control how they perform.

After every competition, discuss how each member contributed to the performance and how the team can improve. Make sure that your squad knows that you are proud of them. It takes a lot of effort to compete and every routine should be a positive experience. Teach them how to deal with their performance on both the good and not-so-good days. Help your cheerleaders to use the scores as a learning tool for the next competition. Cheerleaders must focus on small successes as well as the triumph of winning.

Be a good role model for your cheerleaders at competitions. Sportsmanship is more than just a word; it is an action. At times, you might not agree with the judges' decisions, but do not show your frustration by bad-mouthing the judges. Maintain a positive attitude because your cheerleaders will follow your lead.

Teach your cheerleaders the proper behavior for competitions. Some general rules of behavior are the following:

- Cheer for all teams. They have worked just as hard as your squad.

- Do not make fun of any team.

- Respect the judges and accept their decision graciously. Be a polite winner or loser.

- If your team wins first place, do not stand up and cheer as second place is announced. Let every team celebrate their own placing. Do not steal their limelight.

- Always congratulate the winning team.

- Thank the host school for putting on the competition.

Choreographing the Competition Routine

Create the routine early enough so the cheerleaders have plenty of time to perfect it before they compete. Keep the routine simple, clean, sharp, and safe. Develop a routine that both challenges the cheerleaders and sets them up for success. You need to consider the following issues when creating a routine:

What Category Will Your Team Compete In? Most categories are based on the number of cheerleaders on the team and whether the squad is composed of girls and/or boys. The size of the team competing should be dictated by the quality of the cheerleaders.

What Are the Judges Looking For? Check the scoresheets to know the points available for each of the following categories:

- Continuity and fluid routine. The routine should not have any long gaps where the cheerleaders are not doing anything.

- Difficulty

- Cleanliness

- Synchronization and timing

- Crowd appeal

- Legal and well-done stunts

Will You and Your Team Create the Routine or Will you Hire a Choreographer? If hiring a choreographer, consider the following:

- What is the cost?

- Is music included?

- Will sound effects be added where needed?

- How long will the choreographer spend teaching the routine?

- Will she return a second time to help with details and needed changes?

Be prepared to supply the following information to the choreographer:

- Exact talent and skills of each member (not what you hope they will be).

- Size of your squad.

- Preference in music.

- List of competitions where the team will be competing. This information is important because different areas and companies have different styles.

- Scoresheets from competitions that your team will attend. Some competitions place more emphasis on tumbling, while others award more points on stunting or dancing. The routine should be choreographed based on the competition's scoresheet.

- Rules of the competition: time limit, needed elements, and restrictions.

If you and/or your team are choreographing the routine, consider all the following components:

- Talent of the cheerleaders. Feature the skills that your team has perfected. Don't worry about what they cannot do. Safety, not degree of difficulty, should be your primary focus.

- Composition of the routine. Normally, a routine is divided into three sections: music, cheer, and music. The total music time should never be more than half of the routine. Most routines are a total of two-and-a-half minutes. Needed elements include a variety of jumps, tumbling, sharp arm movements, a crowd-motivating cheer, creative dance, and solid stunts and pyramids. Stay away from story-type cheers. Keep the words simple and easy for the crowd to follow and yell with.

- Music needs to be fast-paced and upbeat. Accentuate with sound effects. Music should appeal to your team and the audience. Music must fit the routine. Incorporate a variety of changes in the music to add interest. Chart the music before you start. Pick out the highs and lows. You can buy premixed cheer music, or cut music yourself with a computer program. Other options are to ask a local DJ to mix a song or to pay a professional company to mix the music. The Internet is a great source for music and companies that cut music.

- Make sure you have elements in the routine that grab the audience and make them say "Wow." Effective attention-getters include a unique pyramid or a sky-high basket toss. Start with a crowd-pleasing beginning and always end the routine with the same excitement.

- Symmetry and patterns. The human eye loves symmetrical moves. Include formation changes, roll-offs, contagions, level changes, complementary movements, and group work.

- Use transitions for a smooth flow from one element to another. Do not stay in the same formation for more than one eight-count.

- Have the cheerleaders move and use as much of the floor as possible to create a visual effect.

- Outline the routine on paper to assist in teaching it to your cheerleaders. List everything in eight-counts.

- Use signs to help lead the crowd in the cheer section.

Once the routine is planned and the music is set, concentrate on perfecting the routine. Team members should do the following:

- Practice all elements to counts.

- Practice the routine as if they are performing.

- Perfect timing and stamina. The cheerleaders need to work as one unit. No one cheerleader should stand out above the rest.

- Break the routine into sections and perfect each section.

- Concentrate on good form in the jumps. Do not sacrifice form for height.

- Make tumbling safe by using proper technique.

- Keep volume loud when cheering. Enunciate every word.

- Use sharp, strong arm movements.

- Practice in front of a mirror and each other.

- Have positive facial expressions that display enthusiasm and confidence. The cheerleaders should look like they are having fun!

Step back and check for dead spots. If something is not working, take it out. The routine should hit most of the time. Do not leave in an element that the team has not perfected or a stunt that does not regularly hit. Remember, the routine must be clean and well-synchronized, with solid stunts, sharp arm movements, and strong tumbling. Videotaping a routine and playing it back for the team to critique is very helpful.

When working on a routine, avoid the following:

- Overused music (If several other teams use the same song, you will lose points on originality.)

- Poor-quality tape or CD

- Movements that are vulgar or highly sexual

- Staying in the same spot for a long period of time

- Slow cheers or movements

- Singing the words of the cheer

- Sloppy moves

- Looking scared, unhappy, bored, etc.

It is up to the cheerleaders to "sell" the routine when performing. Both the audience and the judges want to have fun with the routine and the cheerleaders can make this happen by demonstrating lots of energy and smiles throughout the routine.

Selection of Competitions

Many companies, schools, and organizations offer competitions for cheerleaders. To help you decide which ones to attend, consider the following questions:

- Is the competition run professionally and is it well-organized?

- What is the cost?

- Are mats provided for both the practice area and the performance surface? What is the size of the mats?

- Are the judges certified?

- What is the time limit?

- What elements are needed in the routine?

- What are the category divisions?

- Will the organization send you a copy of the scoresheet?

- What are the date, time, and location of the competition?

- What are the rules?

- Will professional spotters be present?

- How many awards will be given?

Select competitions that suit the style and personality of your team. Consider attending and watching a competition before actually competing in one. Don't take your squad to a national-level competition their first time out. Remember that you want this experience to be a positive, learning event. Investigate all avenues, so your team will be ready to perform at their best and reap the rewards of a job well done.

Coach's Responsibilities at a Competition

- Arrive with the team.

- Verify eligibility and have all the necessary paperwork.

- Set a positive example throughout the competition.

- Be responsible for the conduct of your team.

- Know the rules of the competition.

- Attend the coaches' meeting.

- Have the squad ready to take the floor at the designated time.

- Have the tape or CD properly cued.

- Be prepared to start the music once the squad is on the floor.

- Have a backup tape or CD.

Hosting a Competition Outline

Secure a Facility
- Complete rental form
- Rent mats

Secure a Sound System
- School? Hire? Mikes?

Set Categories and Format

Finances
(Check with school bookkeeper for proper procedures)
- Cost for facility
- Cost for judges
- Cost of spotters
- Cost for sound system
- Cost for trophies
- Cost for teams to enter
- Cost for spectators
- Cost for programs
- Cost for mailing invitations

Invitational Flyer
- Design of invitation
- Format: where, when, cost, categories, deadline to register, late fees
- Liability forms
- Procedure letter to schools (how the meet will be run, including warm-ups)
- Judging procedures
- Directions to school
- Motel accommodations (if needed)
- Copies
- Addresses of schools
- Mailing deadline

Judges
- Panel of judges
- Scoresheets
- Forms from bookkeeper for payment
- Pencils, food, drinks, money

Spotters
- Contact local colleges with cheerleaders, cheer companies, cheer association
- Cost and how many

Emcee
- Hire or volunteer

Trophies
- How many
- Where to buy
- Sponsors to cover the cost

Program
- Design
- Copies

Fundraisers on the Day of the Event
- 50/50 raffle (jar, tickets, salesman)
- Concessions
- T-shirt sales
- Floral sales
- Teddy bear sales
- Raffles
- Video sales

First Aid Box
- Kit
- Ice
- Cell phone and contact information

Miscellanies
- Tables and coverings
- Chairs
- Extension cords
- Signs
- Parking

Figure 11-1

Cheerleading Championships Medical Release & Appearance Form

PLEASE PRINT CLEARLY

Participant Name _____   Participant's Birthdate (mo/day/yr) _____

Participant's Email _____   Participant's Grade _____

School Name _____   Cheer Coach Name _____

Parent or Legal Guardian: _____

I, the undersigned parent or legal guardian, do hereby grant permission for my son/daughter to participate in the _____ Cheerleading Championship tournament.

I further acknowledge and understand and agree that the possibility of physical illness or injury (minimal, serious, and catastrophic) exists and that my son/daughter is assuming the risk of such injury by participating in this tournament. I authorize any representative of _____ or the event to consent to and authorize any necessary medical attention, treatment, surgery, or administration of drugs by qualified and licensed medical personnel for my son/daughter. I understand I will be notified as soon as possible in the event of an emergency. I understand and agree that all expenses of such treatment are my responsibility.

I agree to protect, defend, indemnify, and hold harmless _____, including its owners, directors, officers, employees, and sponsors from and against any and all claims, demands, losses, suits, liabilities, costs, or other damages including court costs and attorneys fees, arising from any injury to, or death of, son/daughter, the undersigned, or any other persons, or damage to or destruction of property arising out of or in connection with any damage to third parties occasioned by, incident to, arising out of, or in connection with my son/daughter's participation.

I understand that _____ produces promotional material about the program. I understand that my son/daughter may be included in videotape or photography taken during this event. I hereby grant _____, its successors, assignees, licensees, sponsors, any television networks, and all other commercial exhibitors the exclusive right to photograph and/or videotape my son/daughter and further to utilize my son/daughter's name, face, likeness, voice, and appearance as part of the event, and in advertising and promotion of the event, without reservation or limitation. In granting this license, I understand that the NBCA and WSCCA are under no obligation to exercise any of its rights, licenses, and privileges herein granted.

Rules/Regulations

•No smoking, consumption of alcoholic beverages, or use of illegal drugs allowed.

•The _____ reserve the right to discipline any participant for unruly behavior or for conduct unbecoming to the event.
•Participants must respect all venue, campus, and facility rules and regulations.
•Participants must obey all rules and regulations set forth by the event.

I have completely read and understand the above release and rules/regulations.

_____   _____
Signature of Parent or Guardian   Signature of Participant

Street Address: _____

City: _____   State: _____   Zip Code: _____

Home Phone: _____   Business Phone: _____

E-mail Address: _____   Medical Insurance Company/Policy: _____

Emergency Contact: _____   Phone Number: _____

Figure 11-2

- Have emergency forms for all participating cheerleaders.

- Have an emergency kit.

Hosting a Competition

Schools often host their own competitions as a fundraising activity or to give other local schools an opportunity to attend a competition nearby. To host your own competition, you need to get permission from your school, have lots of parental help, have space big enough to accommodate a large crowd, and have adequate parking and restrooms.

The key to a successful competition is planning and lots of help (see Figure 11-1). Safety is your primary concern. You need a matted surface for both the competition area and the practice area. Hire only certified, qualified judges and spotters. Have every cheerleader complete a medical and appearance release form (Figure 11-2) prior to attending the event. Arrange for a certified trainer to be present, if possible, and definitely have written emergency procedures.

Send out pre-competition packets that include the rules of the competition, an entry form, the medical and appearance form, a sample of the judging sheet, dates, site, and time of the competition, a map to the facility, a statement of appropriate conduct for coaches, competitors, and parents, an order form for photos and videos, and information about hotels, if needed.

On the day of the event, create an atmosphere of fun and friendship. You want this competition to be a positive experience for everyone participating. Post plenty of signs directing people to the competition location, parking areas, admission/registration desk, warm-up area, concession stands, and restrooms. Place greeters at the front door to show the competing cheerleaders around the facility. Be sure to have plenty of schedules to give to coaches, cheerleaders, and parents.

Run the competition like a pep assembly. Make sure your emcee is enthusiastic and very attentive to both the audience and the participants. Hold fun contests to fill the gaps between performances. Play music before and after the competition. When trophies are awarded, play songs like "Celebration" or the Olympic theme.

12

Season-Ending Responsibilities

"A successful team comes from mutual recognition."

—Anonymous

The bleachers are empty, the games are over, and the cheering is finished for the season. Many memories were made over the year. Now what's left to do? You need to perform the following tasks:

- Inventory equipment.

- Balance cheer account.

- Plan awards banquet.

- Send thank you notes.

- File season information.

- Send a summary of accomplishments.

- Start planning for next year.

- Evaluate your program.

Inventory Equipment

Collect and inventory signs, mascot uniform, cheerleading uniforms (if they are purchased by the school), and any other spirit items. Check for damaged items to see what needs to be repaired or replaced. Compile a list of needs for next season and do a cost analysis. Order new items as soon as you can.

Balance Cheer Account

Be sure the cheerleaders have paid all their bills, from uniform costs to fundraising expenses. Check with your school bookkeeper to confirm that all purchase orders and invoices were paid. Make sure that you have closed out all your fundraisers and inventoried your leftover items.

Plan Awards Banquet

Whether the season was victorious or less than perfect, you must end the year with a bang. The team worked hard and all members need to be recognized for their contributions. The cheerleaders not only work with each other, but also deal with other athletes, fans, teachers, peers, and parents. You need to have an end-of-the-season celebration. You can keep it simple or make it elaborate; the important thing is to honor them for all they have done. Types of banquets include a potluck dinner at the school, a sit-down dinner in a local restaurant, a dessert potluck, a barbecue, dinner at your house, or dinner at one of your cheerleader's houses. Whatever type of gathering you choose, plan the party around a theme, such as one of the following:

- *"Winner's Circle"*—Use checkered tablecloths. Decorate with checkered flags and anything connected to automobiles.

- *"Sands of Time"* or *"Beach Party Bingo"*—Use towels for tablecloths and sand buckets with signs in them for centerpieces. Decorate with beach umbrellas, beach balls, beach chairs, etc.

- *"Spirit Journey"* or *"Passport to Victory"*—Decorate with suitcases, toy trains, cars, and buses. Design scrapbooks with passport covers.

- *"Follow Your Dream"* or *"The Sky Is the Limit"*—Decorate with plastic tubs covered in cloud-print wrapping paper. Put cotton stuffing inside the buckets to make them look like clouds. Play "Over the Rainbow."

- *"You're a Star"*—Decorate with director chairs, stars, movie projectors, clapboards, spotlights. Food menu should include popcorn and other typical movie snacks.

- *"You Are an A-Maze-ing Team"*—Use mazes as decorations.

- *"You Put Your Heart Into It"*—Decorate with hearts.

- *"Many Hats of Cheerleading"*—Decorate with hats that symbolize the different areas in which they participated during the year.

- *"On the Right Track to Victory"*—Decorate with miniature trains and tracks.

- *Jungle Theme* (if the team is the Lions, Wildcats, Tigers, Panthers, etc.).

- *"Unlocking Your Potential"* or *"Keys to Success"*—Decorate with keys.

- *"Building the Best"*—Decorate with hard hats, wooden building blocks, and construction signs.

- *"Together You Created Magic"*—Decorate with top hats, magic wands, wizards, and cauldrons.

- *"One Small Step for Mankind, One Giant Step for the _____ Cheerleaders"*—Decorate using footprints. On each footprint, list an accomplishment of the squad.

- *"You're Outta This World"*—Decorate with globes, outer space items, etc.

- *"Mission: Possible"*—Everyone wears black glasses and trench coats. Play the theme from "Mission: Impossible." Decorate with spy paraphernalia.

Instead of planning your own banquet, you might also consider combining your cheer banquet with the banquet of the sport team for which the girls cheered. It is very rewarding for the cheerleaders to be included with the football team or the wrestling team and to know that they were appreciated, not only by their coach and parents, but also by the athletic teams that they supported. Keep in mind that if you do your banquet with the teams, the time available for your recognition speech might be limited due to the larger number of athletes.

Awards

You will need to order certificates and letters from your athletic secretary for those cheerleaders who have earned them, based on criteria that you set at the beginning of the season. You can also add your own awards to your banquet. Tailor them to your program and make sure everyone receives a special award. After all, they made it through the season; therefore, they must have contributed something positive to the team. For example, a Coach's Choice Award is a great way for the coach to honor someone who may not be the cheerleader with the sharpest moves or best jumps, but who did an outstanding job and was always on time with a smile on her face. The one who didn't have an excuse as to why she couldn't do something and who was always ready to try. Other examples of awards include the following:

- Most Valuable Team Player

- Most Valuable Personality

- Most Improved

- Best Jumper

- Best Stunter

- Most Spirited

- Best Dancer

- Miss Reliable

- Miss Never Quit

If you choose to give yearly trophies and plaques, it can be expensive. Ask your booster club if they will cover all your costs for these awards. Another way to lessen the annual cost is to have a perpetual plaque with individual plates for yearly winners, so you only have to pay for the new engraving each year. Give the winners a certificate.

It is important to give your senior cheerleaders something to recognize all their accomplishments. Small plaques can be purchased for about $10.00 to $15.00. Have their accomplishments engraved on the plaques and/or add a team photo to the plaque.

Don't limit yourself to the traditional trophies and awards. Be creative and have fun. Some possibilities include the following:

- Make a videotape of highlights of your season and give copies to everyone.

- Make scrapbooks for your cheerleaders.

- Give out t-shirts with the team photo on them.

- Give out cheer posters of pictures taken throughout the year.

- Make individual laminated photo placemats.

- Do a slide show.

You want to highlight the season. Say something special about each cheerleader, by name, in your thank you speech. Remember: you want to reinforce the goals, values, and positive events that happened during the season.

Send Thank You Notes

It is very important to remember and recognize all the people that helped you throughout the year. Show your appreciation by writing them a short thank you note. They will greatly appreciate your kind gesture. You are telling them that they are valuable to you and your program. People to remember include the following:

- Custodians

- Transportation department

- Athletic secretary

- Athletic director

- ASB secretary

- Leadership class

- Parents

- Principals

- Teachers

- Local businesses

- Ticket takers

- Students

- Other school cheerleaders

- Other coaches that have helped you

File Season Information

Once you are done with wrapping up your paperwork, having your banquet, and sending out thank you cards, then organize all your notes. Label everything and file it away for future reference. You should have the following:

- Forms from each cheerleader (permission slips, travel forms, emergency forms, athletic eligibility form, uniform payment records, etc.)

- Progression sheets

- Daily practice plans

- Practice notes

- Game plans and notes

- Season plans

- National Federation of High School Spirit Rules Book (It is very important to include this book in your file. A stunt that was legal that year may not be legal the next year. You want to be able to show the rules that you followed, in case anyone says you taught an illegal stunt.)

- Accident reports

- Notes on parent concerns and how you handled the problems

- Records of coaches' training that you received that year

- Financial information (purchase orders, receipts, prior approvals, invoices)

Keep all information for seven years. If anyone questions you about past events, you will have this information and will not have to rely on your memory about what you did and how you handled a situation.

Send a Summary of Accomplishments

Cheerleaders do so much throughout their seasons. Keep your athletic director and your principals informed of these accomplishments. Send them a summary that includes the following information:

- Games that the cheerleaders attended

- Pep assemblies they led

- The number of times they performed at events in the school and at halftimes

- Community service

- Special projects

- Awards received

- Number of competitions they attended and their results

- School spirit projects

- Special treats they gave to the players

- Homecoming activities

Start Planning for Next Year

The more planning and organizing you do at the end of the season, the more time you will have for your family during the summer.

- Set the dates for tryouts.

- Develop the material that will be taught.

- Reserve tryout space.

- Find tryout judges.

- Advertise tryouts.

- Plan summer camp.

- Plan fundraisers.

- Contact your uniform representative and set the date for uniform fitting.

Evaluate Your Program

The end of the season is the time to sit back and look at your program. What worked for you? What didn't work out the way you thought it would? What changes can you make to improve your program for next year? Every program always has room for improvement.

13

Off-season Training

"Winning is accomplished in the preparation phase, not the execution phase."

—Dr. Robert Anthony

Summer is a time for your cheerleaders to have fun, rest, relax, and visit with friends. You want them to stay in shape during this off-season, but how? You could schedule weekly practices, but with family vacations, many cheerleaders are often gone for several weeks at a time. To help them stay fit and keep updated on cheer material, try the following ideas:

- Schedule a summer camp.

- Set up a conditioning program they can do at home.

- Give the cheerleaders videotapes of all the chants, cheers, and dances they need to learn over the summer.

Summer Camp

Camp develops and strengthens needed cheer skills. It is usually a four-day instructional program led by professional instructors. Your cheerleaders learn new cheers, chants, and stunts, as well as school spirit ideas. Two types of camps are available: residential or private. Choose the type that is best for your squad.

Benefits of Private Camp

- Less expensive.

- Team has one instructor that works solely with them.

- You can structure the program to your specifications.

- Team does not have to travel a long distance.

- Squad can go home at night.

Benefits of Residential Camp

- Living together for four days builds team unity and camaraderie and develops better understanding of each other's personalities.

- The instructors, who are usually college cheerleaders, are good role models. They inspire your cheerleaders to work harder. They also inspire cheerleaders to set a goal to become camp instructors.

- Because residential camps have multiple instructors, stunts are demonstrated and cheerleaders can actually see how to do them.

- Teams motivate and challenge each other.

- Individuals learn to cope with everyday situations away from family.

- Your cheerleaders develop friendships with other teams.

- Teams participate in fun and friendly competition.

- Cheerleaders learn leadership skills.

Summer Conditioning Program

At the end of the school year, hand out a copy of an exercise program that the cheerleaders can do at home. The goals of the program should be conditioning, strength, flexibility, and joint range of motion.

Following is a sample conditioning program that you can give to your cheerleaders. It includes both aerobics and strength training. Every workout should start with a warm-up and stretching. On Monday, Wednesday, and Friday, concentrate on strengthening and power. On Tuesday and Thursday, emphasize endurance and aerobics.

Warm-up (Five minutes)

Always start with a warm-up to elevate body temperature, promote blood flow, and prepare the body to work. Warm-up activities include the following:

- Light jogging

- Jump roping

- Non-stop chant movements using both arms and legs

- Any movements using large muscles

Stretching (10 minutes)

Hold each stretch for 30 counts and do not bounce.

Sitting on the floor

- Legs together, straight out in front. Lean forward and pull toes toward body. This stretch works the calves, upper back of the legs, glutes, and lower back.

- Straddle legs, toes pointed, and lean to one side, arm overhead. Reverse. Lean forward in straddle position. Stretches inside thighs, lower back, and front of lower legs.

- Lie on back, and bend knees into chest. Stretches all the back muscles.

- Lie on back, and bend one knee into chest, then open leg out with knee bent. Reverse.

- Diamond stretch. In a sitting position, place soles of the feet together. Press knees to the floor. Stretches inside thighs and back.

- Beauty Queen stretch. Bend one knee and cross it over the other leg, which is extended straight out on the floor. Rotate trunk to opposite side (i.e., if right leg is crossed over left leg, rotate trunk to right). Reverse. Stretches waistline.

- Clasp hands together in front of body and pull forward. Stretches arms and shoulders. Repeat with arms overhead, then lean to one side and reverse. Repeat with arms clasped behind back. Stretches chest and lower back.

- Grab one hand with the other and pull it back, then push it down. Reverse hands. Stretches wrists.

Standing

- Bend leg back and grab foot. Keep knee bent beside other leg. Reverse. Stretches quadriceps.

- Tilt head toward shoulder. Reverse. Stretches neck.

Weight Training (M/W/F)

Keep a chart to track progress. Focus on proper technique and alignment. Do three sets of 10 for every exercise and stretch in between each exercise. Finish with a one-mile jog/walk, then stretch.

Legs (Strength)

The following exercises use body weight to work the legs.

- Standing squats. Feet apart and toes pointing forward (no turn-out, second position plies). Keep back straight, abdomen in tight, knees over the toes. Do not squat any lower than a 90-degree angle.

- Double lunges. Right leg steps forward and both knees bend. Reverse with left leg forward. Alignment is very important on this one!

- Sit on floor and straddle legs, then lift one leg up and down. Do right, then left, then both together.

Abdominals

- Crunches

- V sit-ups

Legs (Power/Plyometric)

- Repeating tuck jumps. Concentrate on height and landing on the ball of the foot first, then putting the heel down.

- Alternating jump lunges. Start with feet together. Jump, landing with right foot forward and right knee bent. Reverse.

Arms, Shoulder, Back, Chest

- Push-ups (chest). Vary from girls' push-ups to boys' push-ups to elevating the feet.

- Dumbbell press (shoulders and chest). Sitting on a bench or chair, hold two dumbbells together at shoulder level with palms facing in. Palms rotate forward as elbows lift up and in line with the shoulders. Return to starting position and repeat.

- Dumbbell shoulder press (shoulders). Standing, start with dumbbells at shoulders and palms facing out. Push weights straight overhead, keeping dumbbells facing forward. Return to starting position and repeat.

- Dumbbell curls (biceps). Keep elbows tucked into waist and palms facing out. Curl weights up towards body, i.e. biceps curl. Return to starting position and repeat.

- Kickbacks (triceps). Put one knee on a bench and the other foot on the floor. Hold one weight in one hand. Place the other hand on the bench to support the body. Bend forward at the waist until the upper torso is horizontal. Lift upper arm and pull it close to the body. Bend elbow into a right angle. Straighten the arm behind the torso (only the forearm should move). Return to starting position and repeat. Reverse arms.

- Dumbbell row (back). Support body weight on a bench as described for the kickback exercise. This time, start with the weight in the hand down to the floor. Pull elbow up and in to torso. Contract the shoulder blades. Return to starting position and repeat. Change to other arm.

- Prone dumbbell fly (back). Lie on back on a bench. Hold one weight in each hand and extend arms out to the side. Bring hands together overhead with palms facing each other and elbow slightly bent. Contract the shoulder blades. Return to starting position and repeat.

Wrist

- Curls. Lay arm and elbow on a table with wrist hanging over the edge, palm facing up. Holding light weights, curl the wrist. Return to starting position and repeat. Change hands.

- Reverse curl. Assume the same starting position used in the basic curl, but with the palm facing down. Start with the wrist bent and extend downward. Return to starting position and repeat. Change hands.

Aerobics and Conditioning (T/R)

Do one hour of aerobics and conditioning (always remember to warm up and stretch first). Aerobics can be dance aerobics, step aerobics, kickboxing, running, or reviewing and performing chant/cheer/dance video. Do anything that gets the heart rate up to a training rate (roughly 16 beats per minute). Be creative.

Videotape of Cheers/Chants and Dances

Before school is over in the spring, videotape a senior cheerleader performing all your chants, cheers, and dances. Add any new material from camp. Distribute copies to all the cheerleaders. Require them to learn the material on the tape by the beginning of your mandatory practices. Give a test on the first day back to practice.

By using all three of the off-season training ideas discussed in this chapter, your team can return in August and spend more time planning the season, perfecting details, and helping the school, and less time learning chants and trying to get back into shape.

14

Fundraising

"Working together works."

—Dr. Rob Gilbert

Between shoes, uniforms, warm-ups, poms, transportation, and competition fees, cheerleading can be costly. Fundraising will help defray the expenses. Two keys to successful fundraising are good planning and imagination. Fundraising is demanding, but with your enthusiasm and with support from the parents, it is well worth the effort. Fundraising provides more than just financial benefits. Through fundraising activities, cheerleaders will gain valuable business knowledge, develop good work ethics, and learn the value of teamwork as they work together for a common cause.

Before starting any fundraiser, first contact your athletic director for approval. Remember that you must complete the appropriate school paperwork (see Chapter 1).

Steps to Successful Fundraising

- Set goals and objectives.

- Make it fun and easy.

- Be specific about what the money will be used for.

- Assign a project chairman. This role is a great way to teach organization, responsibility, and leadership.

- Write detailed procedures and distribute to cheerleaders.

- If distributing merchandise, have cheerleaders sign a contract agreeing to pay for any lost or misplaced items.

- Set a timeline with a start and ending date.

- Keep accurate records.

- Decide on the collection method. Will customers pay up front or when they receive the merchandise?

- If selling merchandise, keep a log.

- Sell items people really want—food is one of the best.

- Offer incentives.

- Publicize.

- Send thank you notes.

Fundraising Ideas

- Raffles (e.g. raffling off the Homecoming football or district/state championship ball)

- Candy sales

- Selling spirit items like stadium cushions, mini-poms, face tattoos, spirit buttons, etc.

- Car washes

- School carnival
- "Dunk a cheerleader" dunk tank
- Fashion show
- Garage sale
- Contest (e.g. guessing the number of mini-poms in a jar)
- Bowl-a-thon
- Babysitting
- Hosting a cheerleading competition (see Chapter 11)
- Photos with a cheerleader or the mascot
- Auction
- Bagging groceries for a day at the local grocery store
- Handing out free samples at grocery stores (The product company pays for the service.)
- Sponsoring a school dance
- Pageants
- Student-faculty basketball game
- Children's birthday parties
- Face painting for the big game
- Calendar sales
- Coupon books
- Talent show
- Wrapping presents at a local store during the holiday season
- Concessions at games
- Flower sales for Valentine's Day
- Coat check at senior prom
- Cheer-grams
- Christmas wreath sales
- Recycling
- Corporate sponsorship
- Team night at a local fast food restaurant (Many chain restaurants will feature a team for the night; the team receives 10 percent of the night's sales.)
- Teaching a mini cheer camp

Mini Cheer Camp

Check with your ASB secretary and athletic director for the proper paperwork needed for this fundraiser. When you host a mini cheer camp, you are actually accomplishing more than just raising money. You are increasing public relations for your squad, providing an opportunity for them to learn through teaching, and exposing the youth of your community to cheer.

Safety should be your number one consideration. Have enough people supervising the camp to handle the number of participants. One high school cheerleader can safely manage 7 to 10 mini cheerleaders.

Organization is the key to planning a successful cheer camp. Start with the following basics:

- What age group is the clinic for?
- Date, time, and location. How many days will the clinic last?
- What materials are needed?
- When and where will the camp participants perform?
- Promotion of the event

Age Group for the Clinic

Kindergarten through sixth grade is a good range to teach. One thing to keep in mind is that the younger they are, the more attention they require, and the more supervision you will need. The easiest age group to work with is second through sixth graders. They are very eager to learn and have good small motor coordination. The kindergarteners and the first graders usually put on the cutest show, so they really are worth the extra time.

Date, Time, and Location

You will need to decide when to have your mini camp (fall or winter). Each season has its pros and cons. In the fall, during football season, you usually have more access to the gyms for practice. The only indoor sport is volleyball, so you are not competing for gym time as much as in the wintertime, during wrestling and basketball season. However, in the winter, the little cheerleaders will be able to perform indoors for either a basketball game or a wrestling match.

Check gym availability for practice sessions. In addition to your school's gym, check with the local elementary schools for the availability of their gyms. Reserve a facility early and complete a rental agreement. Schedule the mini-camp during the week for three or four evenings for an hour-and-a-half, or all day on a Saturday.

Arrange for the camp participants to perform at halftime at one of the high school games. It is really important not to have them perform when you are playing your biggest rival. Plan it for a game when you are not expecting a lot of spectators. Having the mini cheerleaders perform will help increase the attendance at that game and bring in more money for your school. Usually, the mini-cheerleaders receive free admission and the adults pay.

Material Needed for Camp

• First aid kit, phone, and emergency plan

• T-shirts (Contact your local t-shirt supplier to make shirts for all the attendees. This item will be your biggest cost. Usually, shirts are $5 to $7 each, depending on the number ordered.)

• Cheer and dance to be taught (Delegate a couple cheerleaders to choreograph the routines. Remind them that both the music and the moves need to be age-appropriate.)

• Teambuilding games

• Snacks

• Art supplies (if participants will be making a craft)

• Sound system and music

When the mini cheerleaders arrive at camp, check them in and assign them to a high school cheerleader who will be their "buddy cheerleader." Have check-in and check-out attendance sheets for the parents to sign. Do not allow parents to send a note saying their student can meet them in front of the building. Stress that parents must pick up the child from the room in which the camp is held. Send home a letter the first night stating what your expectations are for the camp. Also include information such as what time the mini cheerleaders need to arrive at the game, what they should wear, when they will perform, and where they can be picked up. Document everything you do, from permission slips to attendance to letters home.

Have the high school cheerleaders do warm-ups, stretching, basic cheer moves, and jumps with the participants. Create fun ways to do these activities. Refer to Chapter 6 for ideas. Add in fun games and crafts. Talk to the mini cheerleaders about sportsmanship, being an athlete, maintaining good grades, and being a good citizen. On the last night of practice, have a run-through demonstration on the performance area (e.g., football field or basketball court).

When and Where They Will Perform

Usually, the mini cheerleaders perform their routine at halftime of a football or basketball game. The following people need to be informed of the upcoming special performance:

• The coach of the team whose game you will be performing at

• Band director, color guard advisor, dance/drill team advisor

• Athletic director, principal, and vice principal

• Custodian

• Ticket takers

Talk to the sport coach about your plans. Check with him, the athletic director, band director, color guard advisor, and dance/drill team advisor to confirm the amount of time available to perform at halftime. Coordinate with the custodian to open needed rooms. Rope off a bleacher section for the mini cheerleaders. Give the mini cheerleaders passes so the ticket takers will know to let them in for free.

Promotion of Event

Design flyers that provide the following information, in detail:

- Dates and times of the camp. Stress the ending time to ensure that parents are there on time to pick up their children.

- Price. Keep the price reasonable so a greater number of students can participate.

- What the participants will receive: number of hours of instructions, t-shirt, and free entrance into the game. Also state that only the cheerleader gets in free and that family members must pay to attend the performance game.

- Which game mini cheerleaders will be performing at.

- Ages that can attend.

- Location. Be very specific about both the school and the room.

- Maximum number of participants.

- Sign-ups date, time, and place. Schedule one night for sign-ups. Have plenty of help. Also allow parents to mail in their registration by a certain date. Be sure to include an address on the flyer.

- Names of the high school cheerleaders that are participating in the camp. It helps when parents of the community recognize the names of cheerleaders.

- Parent release form (on the back of the flyer). The release form should state that the parents give their child permission to participate in the mini cheer camp, and that they understand that they are responsible for providing their own medical coverage. Include spaces on the form for the name of the mini cheerleader, her grade in school, phone number, and t-shirt size.

Take the flyer to your school district administrative office for approval for distribution. After authorization, they will tell you the number of classes per school, which will help you decide the number of flyers to print. Send a note with the flyers asking the teachers to hand them out to the students who are interested. Often, if you bundle the flyers into groups, the school district will deliver them to the schools through their school mail system.

By the end of the week, you and your cheerleaders will be exhausted, but you will have finished a great fundraiser and established wonderful public relations with the younger students and their parents. Good luck!

About the Authors

Pam Headridge is currently in her fourteenth year as the head cheerleading coach at Oak Harbor High School in Oak Harbor, Washington. She has been honored as National Cheerleading Coach of the Year, National Federation Interscholastic Spirit Association Section Eight Coach of the Year, and Washington State Cheerleading Coach of the Year. She writes articles for many national magazines, including *The Coach* and *Sporting Kids*. Pam is on the *American Cheerleader* magazine Coaches Council and is often called upon for her expertise. She is the featured speaker on five educational cheerleading videos: *Fundamentals of Basic Stunting, Creating Excitement with Transitional Stunting, Mastering Advanced Stunting, Physical Conditioning for Cheerleaders*, and *Basic Jumping Techniques*.

Pam also is a widely respected public speaker who travels the country talking on numerous topics concerning cheerleading and coaching. A much-desired presenter, Pam addresses a variety of subjects, from how to handle conflict with cheerleaders and parents to fun ways to motivate athletes.

Her team, the Oak Harbor Wildcats, is nationally recognized for their outstanding skills and community service. They were named 1999-2000 National Team of the Year and have won several titles at USA and Power Athletic Nationals.

Pam began her love for cheerleading at Waterloo Junior High in Maryland and continued to cheer throughout high school and college. She was the founder of the Washington State Cheerleading Coaches Association and still remains very active in the organization. She has numerous certifications, including Cheer LTD National Safety and Judges Certification, American Association of Cheerleading Coaches and Advisors National Safety Certification, United Performing Association Judges Certification, American Sports Education Program Coaches Principles Certification, and National Federation of High Schools Education Program in Cheerleading.

Pam and her husband, Bill, reside on picturesque Whidbey Island. They have two grown children, Misty and Stirling.

Nancy Garr is in her sixth year as cheer coach of Ferndale High School in Ferndale, Washington. She is secretary of the Washington State Cheer Coaches Association and also serves as Region One Representative. In 2003, she became a spirit rules clinician for the Washington Interscholastic Activities Association. Nancy is certified in safety by the American Association of Cheerleading Coaches and Advisors. She also completed and passed the National Federation of High School Coaches Education Program. She is a member of the Washington State Spirit Judges Association, National Federation Coaches Association, Washington State Coaches Association, and the Washington State Officials Association. Nancy is also employed as a special education para-educator at Mt. View Elementary, where she has worked for 14 years.

Nancy and her husband, Bill, live in Ferndale, Washington. They have two sons, Robert and Ryan, who attend Central Washington University, and a daughter, Shannon, who is a cheerleader at Washington State University in Pullman, Washington.